T0128558

SALUTE

MAY YOU LIVE ALL THE DAYS OF YOUR LIFE

MARK C. MARINE

Cover Coordinator: Greg Taucher
Cover Design: Ross Chowles
Cover Photo: Tianyi Xie

authorHOUSE®

AuthorHouse™
1663 Liberty Drive
Bloomington, IN 47403
www.authorhouse.com
Phone: 1 (800) 839-8640

Published by AuthorHouse 04/17/2020

ISBN: 978-1-7283-4389-1 (sc)
ISBN: 978-1-7283-4388-4 (e)

Library of Congress Control Number: 2020901206

To Paula,

to whom I send flowers, just so the roses can meet her,

and

Nate, Jessica and Domiona,

for being the sunshine that makes the roses bloom.

FOREWORD

Allegro con brio

Quick. Cheerful. With fire and spirit. This is *Salute!*

I was raised with two guiding principles as North *Stars* … get as much education and experience as you can, as these are two things that no one can ever take away from you. And honestly, while I value all of my educational opportunities - along with those who brought these into frame – it is the life experiences that I honest-to-God, right-hand-up value the most. The ups. The downs. The gains. The setbacks. The bumps, bruises and scars. However, it is the stories that rise out of life experiences that provide the best *learning moments* for all of us. Going all the way back to our days in the "caves" stories have been an incredibly rich source of knowledge, wisdom, traditions, cultural, and most importantly, keeping the fire of the human spirit burning.

Mark is a storyteller. A storyteller extraordinaire. His wit, wisdom and experiences transport each of us to different times, places, passages and moments in life with an amazing, rich imagination. We've been with him at *Dee's Hamburger Stand* in a far less politically correct era. We've been with him in his living room as he scaled sofas, end table and recliners in a single bound. We've spent many a Sunday dinner with him in the Marine family's dining room. And, he gave us a front-row seat for the moment that changed his life: the day he first cast eyes on Paula. His storytelling is seamless. It's art. But most importantly, it's Mark. Unbridled. Unvarnished. And, all served to us with a wink, a smile, a laugh, a lesson and a tinge of the devil-may-care.

It's said that a writer's biggest challenge is overcoming the "dare" ... the *dare* of the blank page staring up at you, and taunting you to begin spreading ink from your prized, bite-mark ridden Bic pen. However, when you're writing about things that really matter to you and are a part of you, the risk of taking that dare and risks on the page that follow really don't matter. Just ask Mark. And this my friends, is how *Salute!* came to pass.

Greg Taucher
Judge Memorial '72

ACKNOWLEDGEMENTS

I just wrote a book and I'll be damned in not finding the suitable words to express my gratitude. Good HELL! This is not the time to get writer's block. Well...after 27 trash bound first drafts, it finally dawned on me; the only way for me to say thank you is to tell you the story. As you will read in the book, making my point with a story, is in my nature.

Here is the story that caused my soul to be filled with gratitude.

After I had bid my fond farewell to all those wearing a cap and gown at my high school graduation day in 1972, I assumed I would never see most of my classmates again until a future class reunion. Since my life's menu at the time only offered conflicts between career and family, I never participated in any of my class reunions. I felt "shame on me" for reducing my high school reminiscing to a quick "thumb through" of my boxed-up yearbooks.

Then presto! On November 15th, 2019, 47 years after we had graduated, I received an email from a high school classmate of mine, who I knew from our class time together, but, really didn't "hang with," or "pal around" with, outside of the school day. After all, back then, he was one of the cool guys. One of the smart guys - who always got straight A's. He was a good-looking kid - tall, athletic, physically fit, and handsome. He was the funny guy – quick witted, with a deep throated laugh. Yet, the nicest guy – always offering a kind word and gesture. A guy, who somebody like me was envious of, because of his good fortune of being, "That Guy."

Greg Taucher is his name.

A couple of years ago, through the magic of social media, Greg and I had reconnected, and it did not surprise me, he hadn't changed a bit. To my delight, Greg had been reading a few of my stories. He consistently made nice comments about the stories I had written, and eventually, he ramped up his compliments into a stern and demanding encouragement to me; "Write the "FRICKING" book!"

Greg Taucher is not only the man who motivated me to get "off the dime," and "shift it into gear," to write this book. He compiled a superstar team of talent to champion the art work for the front and back covers of this book. Greg combined his acumen in genius, with the brilliant Mr. Ross Chowles, and the skilled and smart Ms.Tianyi Xie, people to this day, I have never met or even talked to, but now feel a kinship to, because of their generous contributions to Greg Taucher's masterminded plan to get my ass in gear.

During the time Greg was singing my praise, other friends also chimed in with encouraging comments as well. And while I was reflecting their tones of cheer, I found myself thinking, "Oh God! Maybe I can write a book!" But without fail, my mind would travel back and forth between the meandering thoughts of becoming a "Best Seller," to my safe zone of procrastination, always retrieving to that defeatist thought of, "Who am I kidding?"

Then it happened, on November 15th, 2019, to be exact. I was informed to what was going on behind the scenes in Greg Taucher's trifecta of talent. Do you know that saying, "What a difference a day makes?" Well, here's the email I read over my morning cup of coffee, starting a chain reaction of difference making days.

Good Afternoon Mark.

Well, it's taken a while to get this on the rails, however, it is on the rails. Ross Chowles, a guy I teach with is a hell of a creative (art director), started a kick-ass agency in South Africa, sold it, and decided to move to the US. to teach, is now on this project. In addition to teaching together, Ross and I are partners in an ad agency in East Lansing, so I have a lot of time for Ross. We're having a shit ton of fun.

What I'd like to get from you is a list of "things" that have been, or you see as foundational in making you and your writing "you." Here's the kicker: these "things" need to be simple and singular enough to lend themselves to a clean/simple illustration. Also, what is your adult beverage of choice?

Thanks. The brains are lit .....
Tauch

WOW! Excitement rushed into my brain led by one of my most favorite Greg Taucher sayings..."You know Mark, sometimes even a brain fart turns out to be something."

So, I sent him my list... and the word, "SCOTCH."

Usually, time will dampen even my most fervent excitement, but even after a few weeks, I was still floating around, dancing on cloud nine in my own little world. Just as I grew accustom to settling back into my daily routines, just like that... Greg's next email changed the game and made me shift the gears.

Hello Mark,

"In my 30+ years in "adbiz/showbiz" the one thing I learned is that every "idea" starts with a blank sheet of paper .... well, Ross Chowles and I started with a blank sheet of paper.

We took your "list" (Word doc); went to Dagwood's (a dive bar just off the Michigan State campus); ordered some "brown water;" kicked around some ideas and lines; and then Ross + Tianyi Xie (a very talented graphic designer and photographer we work with) went to work.

The ice cubes in the glass represent moments we highlighted from your list - legs, ladder, baseball, etc. (we'll need to finalize, of course). But the ice cubes, aren't really ice cubes ... Ross and Tianyi are planning to hand mold and shape the "cubes" using clear acrylic resin. Never done it before, but we figured it would be a fun weekend DIY project if things come to fruition. Hey, never be afraid to suck at something new!!

At any rate, you have a "cover idea" for your book. "Write a the "FRICKING" Book!"

Best,
Tauch

Whoa! There it was! The front and back covers to a book I hadn't even written yet. I was almost in tears. What a nice thing to have happen to me. "This art work is unbelievable! It's perfect!"

And who are these people, Ross Chowles and Tianyi Xie? How did I get so lucky?

Then it hit me. "Oh my God!" I sighed. I've got to "Write the *"FRICKING" Book!"*

I send my heartfelt thanks to you, Greg Taucher, for your constant and enthusiastic encouragement. And to Ross Chowles, and Tianyi Xie, I will always stand in awe that you, along with Greg, shared your gift of talent on me, someone you didn't even know. I'm telling you, "People are going to buy this book just for the cover!"

And to all of my friends out there, you know who you are, that also continued to cheerlead me by dropping me a comment or two, saying something to the tune of, *"Write the "FRICKING" Book!"* I say my most sincere THANK YOU! You built my confidence to the point I decided to give it a try. The world is a better place because of you. You are the people who are the ones who want to develop and lead others. And what makes it even better, is, you are those unique people who share the gift of their time and talent to encourage those of us who are unsure. Thank you to all of you! You, the very ones who strive to grow and help others grow too, I say. *"SALUTE!"*

INTRODUCTION

There I laid, in a ditch, frenzied; desperately trying to organize any leftover rational pieces of my mind, trying to make sense of what just happened.

"God it's cold," I thought.

What just happened?

Then, without provocation, just like in the early morning of that day when this nightmare began, I fell back into darkness, unconscious to my plight.

I have heard of those stories when people say their lives flashed before their eyes just as they think death is inevitable. It's those precious seconds right before they think they are going to die when, by surprise, BAM! Their whole life shows up in their brain, running fast forward on the 10X speed, to get it all in before that one last final heartbeat.

But it didn't happen that way with me. My mind must have known that even though I thought I was knocking on death's door, the *Grim Reaper* wasn't home that day.

Instead, I survived being abducted.

And having passed out from not being able to breathe through the dirty black bag they put over my head, then finally finding my way out of that ditch to live another day, the stories that have most influenced my life, have slowly and surely, at the damndest times, popped into my brain.

It's my life "slothing before my eyes."

I propose a "*toast*" to all of you . . .

"May you always tell your stories!"

No ditch needed.

"SALUTE!"

MY WHITE PRIVILEGE

"No one has been barred on account of his race from fighting or dying for America, there are no white or colored signs on the foxholes or graveyards of battle."

John F. Kennedy

I was 8 years old, standing with my parents and brother, 5th in line, at the original *Dee's Hamburger Stand* on 3500 South in Granger, Utah. Nothing stirred the appetite of a youngster like the bigger than life, round faced clown, holding multiple colors of balloons, which seemed to be shouting; "Everything on this menu is bad for you to eat."

This was pre- McDonald's empire days, pre- sitting inside to eat, days, and pre- drive thru days. You simply waited in line, took your turn at the window, got your order, then either walked or drove away, arguing where you were going to go to eat the thing.

There, ahead of us in line, in lily white Granger, was an African American gentleman waiting patiently for his turn to order. Being Sunday afternoon, all were dressed in their church going outfits. It was a beautiful, peaceful, comfortably warm Spring day. And I was just happy to be out of church. That is, until some smart aleck teenager waiting in line behind us said to his friend;

"Look, there's a (N- word!)"

I chuckled.

But immediately the smile jumped off my face as my 6 years older than me brother, grabbed my arm with a death grip, looked at me, asking silently with his shocked, wide eyes, "Are you crazy?"

I was confused, because I had heard this word at school, didn't know better, and thought, this was par for the course. My grade school, 1st grade through 8th, was a medley of first-generation ancestry from around the globe. Commanded by women of faith, we we're taught that unconditionally, we all were the same.

Yet, on the playground:

Me and my Italian friends were "*wops*" and "*dagos.*"
My Mexican friends were "*spics*" and "*wet backs.*"
My Chinese friends. . . "*chinks*" and "*tight eyes.*"
My Japanese mates, "*japs.*"
My Irish pals, "*mick.*"
My German friends, "*krauts.*"
And my black buddies were, well . . . you know.

And of course, "*4 eyes*" if you wore glasses.

After recess, we ate together, prayed together, and made plans for weekend sleep-overs. We all were the best of friends. A group of guys who didn't know we were different from each other, because, in our hearts and souls, we weren't. We had no idea that our friendly nicknames had consequences.

Back at Dee's . . .

Although I am certain the black gentleman was too far ahead in line for him to hear what was said, or hear my whispered chuckle, my Mom grabbed my right arm, my Dad my left, and lifted me up off the ground, tugging so hard, I was moments away from being a turkey wishbone, ready to be split in two, with no apologies for the damage. I was in big trouble, and for that split second of not knowing why, I really didn't have time to ask what was going on?

Before I knew it, there I was, flanked by my parents, brother to the side, standing front and center to this towering, top hat wearing, matching handkerchief in top suit pocket, dapper, distinguished black man, who was soon not to be a stranger.

My Mom did the talking: "Sir, my sons would like to hear your story. Please, pass on eating burgers today for lunch and do us the pleasure of you, and your family in the car, coming to our house to eat." He must have known my Mom never took no for an answer, so . . . they did.

Thinking back, I'm certain this man, who we knew for less than two minutes, got the gist of what my parents were doing. I could tell he was all in, proving my long-held belief that the parents of my childhood's generation were all, without question, on the same page.

Italian lunches really aren't lunch; they're the *Christmas Buffet* at a luxury resort hotel. Preparation time is considerable. Just enough time for a life lesson. As my Mom cooked, my Dad moderated a round table with no round table in our house. My Dad asked, "Please tell us what the "*N- word*" means to you." The man, his wife, and 4 year old daughter, with pained expression, rolled out story, after story, after story; for over an hour.

That day changed everything. The innocence of ignorance was now gone. I could not say anymore that I should have known better.

I knew better!

And now I cringe every time I hear, even in jest, a racial slur. As if I just learned about sex for the first time, I felt I joined the world of people that knew better too.

Then . . . 10 years later, it happened to me, a magnified cringe.

"*Black Like Me*"

I tan really easy. And I tan really dark. During the height of the baseball season, I looked like a *Hershey Bar* with an *SOS* steel wool soap pad on top. Curley hair and dark skin. I loved it!

Made me better looking than I really was.

Back in the day, at a time when I thought I could throw a baseball through the car wash and never get it wet; I was pitching in what was to me, the most important game of my young career. This was a big fish in a small pond kind of deal. Non-the-less, it was my pond.

Athletes always have a *Shakespearean* type of conflict to struggle with. On the field there's the necessity to have a one-upmanship swagger that clearly states: "I'm 10-foot-tall and bullet proof." Yet, out in the real world, athletes need to leave that posture behind to mimic *Mother Teresa.*

Every time my love of baseball took control of my ego, transforming me into an arrogant *ass wipe*, my Father's voice would sneak into the back door of my brain, thrusting its way to my conscience. I'd hear his raspy voice saying, "Hey big shot! There's a billion people in China that don't give a shit!"

Anyways . . . We won! Yea for the home team!

As every athlete knows, after the shower, the interviews, and the high fives, you catch yourself counting down the hours until the morning paper was to be delivered in order to see what the sport's guys had to say about your performance. In college, no one wakes up early on the weekend. But not me! Not on that Sunday. I craved to see what the critics had to say. And most important, were the scouts impressed?

At the crack of dawn, I beat the newspaper boy to the local gas station. Nervously tapping my foot in anticipation, there I waited with just enough money to buy a paper, not just for me, but one for my Mom, Dad, brother, girlfriend, a homeless guy, and the dog.

This was a BIG deal for me!

Finally, the paper boy arrived. I bought all 10 copies. (it was a small gas station) As if I were a Hollywood star waiting to see what *Siskel & Ebert* had to say, I hurriedly turned to the Sport's Section.

There it was!

Front page!

A quarter page picture with the caption . . .

"Mark Marine, Colored Pitcher for The Home Team Gets the Big Win."

REALLY???

Of all the defining characteristics to choose from, the color of my skin got top billing? And I'm a white guy in December! My African American heritage is manufactured by the sun. And I wear it well. But even to this day, being darker than you, I have never figured it to be a defining characteristic.

The headline stupefied me. How could the word "*colored*" still be used as a defining characteristic in 1974? After all, we were the generation of *Woodstock*. We collected post cards from *Haight Asbury* and played "*Give Peace a Chance*" on a continuous loop. Love was in the air!

I remember how my African American teammates and I laughed about the newspaper article.

My black friends thought it was funny, kidding me that now, more girls would dance with me because, one, they would think I had rhythm, and two, well . . . you'll figure it out.

And let me say, in February during Spring training when I hardly had a tan line, not once did the headlines read: "*Mark Marine the White Pitcher.*" It was always "*Right Hander,*" or "*Rookie,*" and when I couldn't find the strike zone, "*Scatter Arm.*" Never "*Honky,*" "*Whitey,*" or "*Cracker.*"

Later, after graduation, I was still chasing my dream. That's when I learned having a dark tan proved its value to my white privilege.

Two years later, there I sat in the bullpen, a place set aside for pitchers to be sequestered from the other players who were pissed off that we only had to work every four days. With an ice bag strapped to my right wing, I was daydreaming about my night dreams when I heard the voice of the usher. I look twelve feet up, and there, hanging over the railing, yelling, with a smirk on his mouth, "Hey, number 26! A gal in *Section C* wants me to give you this!" Then he threw down an envelope that traveled as if it was full of rocks.

Inside, a room key from the *Denver Hilton* and a handwritten note which read: *"I'm a cutie and would love to see the white parts so I can appreciate the tan."*

You could see my *"HAPPY DANCE"* from the cheap seats!

And after all these years, that has always been my favorite *"White Privilege."*

MY TOY STORY

My favorite toy in 1960 was an old, oversized, discarded pillowcase which I fetched out of the garbage and colored a big red "S" on its back so I could play *Superman*. I loved playing *Superman*, making myself the hero of the day.

As a 5-year-old, my only "me time" of the week would happen every Saturday morning. My parents and older brother would sleep in, and I would rule the roost. There was no oversight, no people older than me hovering to tell me my next move. Just me and my brain trying to fit all this freedom into the little time before everyone would wake. I could eat the things I shouldn't, explore forbidden drawers, and best of all, the TV had an audience of one; ME!

Saturday morning television was the best! With a whopping 3 channels to pick from, the deliberation in my brain of what to watch was pure joy. I always chose the same three shows. One right after the other.

'*Yogi Bear*',
'*The Flintstones*',
and my favorite, '*Superman*'.

There I would sit, crossed legged, 3 feet away from the TV. With a *Hershey Bar* in one hand, *Tootsie Roll* in the other, I thanked God I wasn't dead because Heaven couldn't be this good.

After just saving the world from evil doers for the last 26 minutes, right at the time when *Superman*, now *Clark Kent*, was straightening his tie and adjusting his glasses to carry on small talk with *Lois Lane*, the rest of the *Marine* clan would slowly wake and start to invade my space.

DAMN! I hated my me time coming to an end.

My Mom always started her morning in the kitchen cooking breakfast and starting that night's dinner pasta sauce. My Dad started his days with his usual, shit – shower - shave routine. And my older brother? Well, he would always pull the covers back over his head until the "*breakfast is ready*" alarm was voiced loudly by my mom.

My me time was soon to be over.

Although I had never done it before, and I knew deep down it was a big NO-NO, the motivation of the "cool" of *Superman*, combined with the energy from a sugar overload, I figured it was time to fly. I grabbed my "S" marked pillowcase from its special shelf in my toy closet and strapped it on as a cape, stood on the edge of the couch, jumped as high and as far as I could, arms extended, squealing out "*SUPERMAN*!" I transformed myself into *Superman's* mini me. Landing safely on the soft cushions of the couch, the trampoline bounce back effect was icing on my happiness cake. Just like a black lab playing fetch, I scrambled back to the arm rest of the couch and did it again and again.

But it was my Mom who had the superpower of x-ray vision that day.

Without leaving her station at the stove, wearing her kitchen curtain styled dress and an apron, she saw with the eyes in the back of her head, straight through the wall separating the kitchen and living room, exactly what I was doing. With a tad of anger in her voice, she yelled out her command . . .

"QUIT IT MARK, YOU'RE GOING TO BREAK SOMETHING AND GET HURT!"

I yelled "Ok Mom!" But since I was already mounted on the arm rest of the couch, I squatted like a pooping camper and sprung my legs with all my might . . .

Oh the height!
Oh the distance!

I too could jump tall buildings in a single bound. Be faster than a speeding bullet. More powerful than a locomotive.

Look!
Up in the sky!
It's a bird!
It's a plane!
It's Superman!

Yes, I was *Superman!* That strange visitor from another planet who came to earth with powers and abilities far beyond those of mortal men. *Superman*, who can change the course of mighty rivers, bend steel in his bare hands. And who, disguised as *Clark Kent*, mild-mannered reporter for a great metropolitan newspaper, fought the never-ending battle for truth, justice and the American way.

In my mind, right then and there, in midair, that would be me!

Then this happened.

I overshot the length of the couch by half. I hit the end of the couch squarely, right on my hip line. The bottom half of me went one way, while the top half of me turned the other. Looking like a cat twisting to get all 4's down, *Murphy's Law* took control, and just like a piece of toast, there was no way I was going to hit bottom butter side up.

Fun turned into panic as the corner of my mom's prized glass Italian style coffee table broke my fall right above my right eyebrow.

OUCH!

The owie wasn't that bad, but the blood was. The cut above my eye looked like a full ketchup bottle squirting its contents like a 4x4 just ran over it.

SHIT!
Think fast!

My mind raced with panic. "Please God, let me die if I broke the table." And don't bleed on anything! Whoa! Mom didn't hear it! Thank you Jesus! Good! I'll go show Dad, he never gets mad.

I ran down the hall, hand covering my wound, trying to keep blood from getting on anything but me. I turned the corner into the bathroom where my Dad was in the third phase of his morning trilogy, the shaving part. I didn't say a word, made eye contact, and took my hand away from the cut.

My Dad always shaved with one of those old-style *Gillette* razors. You know the kind. A *Samurai Sword* type blade that could cut through a building block with one swoosh. Caught by his blind side, my Dad's knee jerk reaction to my blood squirting forehead resulted in him literally cutting his throat as he was just starting to work on the neck stubble of his shave.

Great, more Blood!

Quick! How do we not only stop the bleeding, but most important, contain it without using Mom's good towels?

At this point, let me say how I have always admired my father's resourcefulness and ability to improvise under pressure. He was a *MacGyver* type of guy. With the same concern as me, don't make a mess, he grabbed a *Kotex*, pressed it up against his neck, slapped one in my hand to be used for my head, and drove me and him, one handed, in his stick shift *Buick*, to the doctors.

The good news is the cuts weren't serious. But they were strategically located in just the right place on our bodies to maximize the flow of blood. Although we looked like the "*Texas Chainsaw Massacre*" going in, it was just a couple of stiches for each of us going out.

When we got home, breakfast was ready and waiting, and Mom was pissed.

As we walked through the front door my Dad said to both me and my brother, "Don't say a word, not a peep, not until your mom speaks first. And <u>DON'T</u> say something stupid." In dead silence, shuffling like the cast of the *Walking Dead*, we sat down at the table to eat.

"I TOLD YOU SO!", my mom yelled.

(enter a long and awkward silence)

"Well Mark, do you anything to say?", my Mom asked.

Yes, I said:
"Mom, what's a Kotex?"

GOD LOVES BASEBALL TOO

Baseball was king at our house. My Dad loved the game and my Mom loved to watch me and my brother act out the tutoring of my father. In 13 years, my parents never missed a game.

In a home where organization skills ran wild, things got rearranged for baseball. Schedules were adjusted. Mealtimes were changed. Even house cleaning chores were delayed when needed. All to accommodate the diamond.

The only other thing that came close to bumping a scheduled activity off the calendar was *Mass*. We could never miss *Mass*.

So, with two boys, six years apart in age, me playing in the *Granger Little League*, my brother in the *Granger Babe Ruth League*, and C.Y.O. (*Catholic Youth Organization*) baseball at two different parks on Sunday, it was a miracle we never missed a game.

Thank God for a full menu of *Sunday Services* at our Parish, because I swear, my Mom would have called the Pope to get it changed if there was an undoable conflict between God and game. But Jesus and the "*Play Ball*" call of the umpire always seemed to work itself out.

It was hard for me to get into trouble when baseball was involved. I could push the limits of my parent's patience. If I had a bat, ball, and glove in hand, "just a minute" could finally be an acceptable answer.

Except on this particular Saturday.

Every 4 years, right on schedule, my Dad set out to paint the outside of our house. Although there was a continuing deliberation, the same light green color with white trim was never to be changed. I think it is still that same light green color 55 years later.

Playing catch with my next-door neighbor friend, Steve, was by today's standard, my addictive video game. So when Steve showed up with his mitt, it was game on.

Four throws in, and we hear my Dad, paint brush in one hand and a gallon of *Sherwin Williams* paint in the other, bark out like a third base coach, "Don't play here, I'm painting." Steve started to walk off, but I waived him back holding the posture of, "it's ok," and tossed him the ball.

Two more flings and I hear in a louder, almost angry voice, "Goddamit MARK! Play somewhere else!"

"OK Dad," I sadly said. I figured I do one more hurl and then we would go play in Steve's yard. I might as well end it with my best fast ball. A high hard one, I thought.

I wound up, opened up my stance, had perfect form, let go of the pitch, and let her fly. It looked to be a perfect strike when God, with the axiom of, "I'm on your Dad's side," guided my brand new, perfectly white, red seamed baseball, with a 90-degree turn, straight into the bucket of green paint.

SWISH! Nothing but net! I couldn't have done it at *The County Fair* for a stuffed animal.

The green paint splashed everywhere. On the bushes, on the white trim, on my Dad's pants and shirt, there was even splatter on his face.

Holy crap!

I screamed the *"F"* word, not caring at all that if my Mom heard it, she would not break stride, and grab the bar of *Ivory Soap* to be used for my mouth wash. This was bad! And I knew it.

I dropped my mitt and the ball, my Dad dropped the paint brush, and the chase was on. I ran in the front door, turned down the hall, and headed toward the safety of the underside of my bed. But as I passed the hall closet, *Satan*, not to be left out of the fun, grabbed my hand and made me swing the hall closet door open in an effort to slow down my Dad's pace.

That was a big mistake!

Being blindsided by a cheap, track home, closet door, my Dad barged through, leveling the door to the floor, hinges and all. The *Incredible Hulk* hadn't been invented yet, but that day my Dad became the prototype. With shades of green all over him, and with rips in his shirt and pants from his expanded muscles, he lifted the bed, mattress, and box springs up and away as if he were moving a small TV tray. He picked me up by my shoulders from what you would recognize as a fetal position, but what in truth was a laying on the ground, praying position, and plopped me sitting straight up on the bed he just moved six feet away.

My Dad had never spanked me up to this point in my life, that was always left to my Mom and her spatula, but I was sure I was going to get it this time. Maybe even the belt.

"Please God, get me out of this one. I promise I will be good forever from now on," I prayed.

But, after his teeth ungritted, his eyebrows went back to normal, and the grip on my shoulders lightened, my father, the ever present baseball man said, "You better learn how to control your fast ball if you want to be a pitcher," turned around, and went back to painting.

Whoa! God loves baseball, too!

Years later, playing *Babe Ruth Baseball*, I was on the mound to pitch on the same day they were painting the adjacent pavilion out in deep right field. Nauseated by the flashback of painting days gone by, I couldn't find the strike zone that day either.

NO! THAT'S MINE!

Just like you, I was groomed as a baby to believe the world revolved around me. Endless cuddles, constant kisses, food when I cried, and never having to hold a pee or poop. Life was good!

That is, until the day I was introduced to the word *share*.

I remember the angry tears I shed the day my Mom suggested I split my *Hershey Bar* in half and give that part of my treat to my neighbor friend, Steve. I was crying because any suggestion made by Mom was never really a suggestion. It was a drill sergeant's order in disguise, never up for discussion.

This was MY candy bar, bought and paid for with MY allowance.

Not yet old enough to know the appropriate swear word but experienced enough to know a tantrum would cancel that night's dinner's dessert, I broke the bar in exact, equal parts. I forced my arm to extend, and in remiss, made myself pry my hand open while seeing the happiness of making Steve's day. I was pissed at a time when I didn't even know what being pissed off was.

I guess it showed on my face that I wanted to be mad at Steve for being in the wrong place at the wrong time, because my Mom said, just like yours has said so often, "Knock that sneer off you face or I'll knock it off for you."

Ten minutes later, I was fine. Steve and I, with chocolate on our lips, skipped off to gather other friends to play hide and seek.

A few years later, it was my Dad's turn to do the dirty work of teaching me how to divvy up what I thought to be only mine. Apparently, a pre-nuptial treaty was signed between my Mom and Dad stating that, "At the first sign of testosterone," the teachable moments of sharing became the duty of the father.

Even though they both agreed about the necessity of amending my personal constitution when needed, the way each of them made their point could not have been more polarized.

My Mom would take the oxygen out of the room, make me believe she really did have eyes in the back of her head, and had me praying to God she didn't imagine that glazed look in my eyes was the forming of an attitude that would bring out the wooden spoon. My Dad, not so much. He was a, *"wax on - wax off,"* type of guy. It was like being raised by *Carol Burnett* and *The Dalai Lama.*

Sharing candy was one thing; the lesson of sharing time was introduced to my disposition on a Saturday morning in 1965.

There I was, excited and fully prepared to settle in and participate in my favorite family weekend routine of watching *"The Yankee Game of the Week"* in tandem with all the chores that could be done within earshot of the TV. Between 1964 and 1974, *CBS* owned the *Yankees*. There was never not a Saturday, *"Yankee Game of the Week."* Mantle, Maris, Berra, and Ford became my life long best friends.

Just as *Mickey Mantle* stepped into the batter's box, my Dad announces, "C'mon Mark, were going to go mow the *'Ward'* lawn." (A "Ward" is the Mormon version of what Catholics call a Parish)

WHAT???
WHY???
SHIT!!! (the shit part was under my breath)

"Let's do it tomorrow!" I bellowed out. When that didn't work, I tried, "We're *Catholic*!" And, "Why are we mowing the *Mormon's* lawn?" You love the *Yankees* more than me!" Finally, I moaned, "Are we converting?"

For the first time in the decade I had lived, my Dad spoke in his loudest and most stern voice . . . "You can't mow *Mormon* grass on Sundays!"

So off we went. My Dad pushing the lawn mower, and me, dragging the rake, broom, and trimmer like I was playing tug-o-war with the asphalt. The one block distance up to the *Granger Mormon 6th Ward* became my Dad's pulpit.

"Look," he said; "Everybody takes their turn mowing the church lawn . . . "It's our turn now," he said with a smile. And that was that.

The next day, with no *Yankee Game* on TV, we mowed the *Catholic* grass at our house.

Then there was this. The sharing of money.

After actually paying attention in my high school civics class earlier that day, I couldn't wait to make my argument about taxes over my family's traditional Tuesday night, candy bars for dessert, dinner.

All the way home on the school bus, I rehearsed with my classmates our conclusion that all our parents were being screwed by the government by having to pay taxes for a school system that none of us would ever use. After all, we were all kindergarten to senior high, parochial school, tuition paying students. None of us would ever experience the pleasures of a public school. I even prepared a, *"Here's how we can spend the money,"* list.

Over spaghetti, meatballs, and a basinet sized basket full of garlic bread, I started my dissertation. Just shy of hollering, I said, "So why do you guys have to pay taxes for the public-school system that we will never use?!" I continued on,

"What a joke!"
"It's totally unfair!"
And what about this?

And what about that?
Yadda, yadda, yadda!

With no rebuke, or questions for clarity, while still twirling his spaghetti onto his fork, my Dad, in the tone of, this should be obvious, said: "Mark, get out of the shallow end of the pool! Good hell, how many games do you think you'll win if you're the only one that knows the plays? Your education will be meaningless surrounded by ignorance."

Then in a, *"Fredo, you broke my heart"* moment, he finished, "I never want to hear you complain again about my money, or yours, going towards helping someone else."

Well, that shut me up.

My 16-year-old brother said, "Here, take half of my *Hershey Bar*." The one and only time my Mom ignored the smirk on his face.

CLEANLINESS NEXT TO GODLINESS

Long before child rearing had the cute catch phrase of *"helicopter parenting,"* the moms and dads of my childhood employed *"time outs"* and *"grounded"* as their way to hover over our misdeeds.

But not at my house!

No, Italian Catholic mothers rectified every behavioral problem by prescribing janitorial duties and a prayer.

When I was 7 years old, I got caught stealing a piece of bubble gum during a time when penny candy actually cost a penny. My mom blew a gasket, throwing a fit in rant and rage.

With no driver's license or a car, and wearing her *"Donna Reed"* house dress and high heels, she grab my right wrist, started her tongue-lashing, and proceeded to drag me back to the scene of the crime in an embarrassing and humiliating 2 block *"perp walk"* through the neighborhood to the *Safeway Grocery Store*. The tears of shame rolling down her cheeks prevented me from daring to even say a word.

After I apologized to:
the *manager*,
cash register clerk,
the *produce guy*,

the *meat counter guy*,

the *baggers*,

and every person shopping at the time, my Mom, the *Honorable Judge Josephine*, handed down my sentence. It was a twofold punishment.

First, with the enthusiasm of an *Olympic Curling Brush Master*, I would spend each and every day of my 3-month summer vacation broom sweeping the parking lot of the store.

Then, apparently there was not enough God in my life. So of course, as every Catholic guilt spreading mother does, she required me to carry her rendition of a criminal's ankle bracelet . . . a Rosary in my pocket at all times.

To this day, I have never stolen another thing. I still have the Rosary, and I'm not a big fan of bubble gum. After that incident, most of my moral misdemeanors were remedied with a couple of "*Our* Father's" and a dust mop.

That is, until this . . . A blue ribbon, you are going to Hell, religious felony. Truly a *Mortal Sin!*

Here's what happened.

My best friend was running to be a *Student Body Officer* at the all-boys, Catholic High School where we were enrolled. I was his campaign manager. The most important day of the campaign was *"SKIT DAY."* All candidates were allowed to present a 7-minute skit to an overcrowded, standing room only, assembly. The perfect opportunity to weave a little lighthearted sarcasm into the boring politics of a school election.

We chose a breakfast scene out of the popular sitcom television show, *"Leave it to Beaver."*

(*Leave It to Beaver* is an American television sitcom about an inquisitive and often naïve boy, Theodore *"The Beaver"* Cleaver, and his adventures at home, in school, and around his suburban neighborhood. Along with his parents Ward and June, and his brother Wally, the show attained an iconic status in the United States, where the *Cleavers* exemplified the ideal suburban family of the mid-20th century.)

Our one act play starts at the *Cleaver* kitchen table where our candidate, *"The Beaver,"* would voice his complaints about the school.

The action opens up on a school morning with June Cleaver wearing her apron, busily cooking breakfast, as her husband, Ward Cleaver, and their son Wally, sit at the breakfast table talking about what Dad was reading in his morning paper. But where's the *"Beaver?"*

Suddenly, *"The Beaver"* comes rushing down the stairs in full school uniform, with little dabs of toilet paper stuck on his chin, cheek, and neck. *"Beaver"* had decided to shave for the first time. With Ward and Wally dazed in the confusion of why a shave was needed, the smart aleck remarks started forming on their lips. But Mom was there to save the day. With orange juice in one hand, June walks over to little Theodore and gently strokes the back of her hand across the left cheek of her youngest son and declares . . .

"Why Ward!!! My Beaver's getting hairy!"

With a standing ovation, the entire male student body erupted in boisterous laughter.

Later that afternoon in the demerit office, my Mom, Dad, and the Nuns, seemed not to know where to begin. At first, my Mom and the Nuns didn't get the joke. I could tell my Dad got the joke but put on a face of discouragement, acting like he was peeved. But I could tell there was a poop eating grin hidden beneath his dismay.

Once the joke was explained, and my Mom checked for *666* tattooed under my hairline, I was in line for a world of hurt. When the *"how could you"* shock left my mom's lecture, the penalty list started to fill up. I had to wash the walls, toothbrush clean the tiles, and spit shine the woodwork in the 2800 square foot, 8-bedroom, 4-bathroom, convent.

When I timidly asked, "Is there anything else?" Altogether, without a blink, growled out, "GO TO CONFESSION!"

My confessional penance from the priest? Back-to -back- to- back, *Novenas*.

Novena (from Latin: novem, "nine") is an ancient tradition of devotional praying in Christianity, consisting of private or public prayers repeated for nine successive days or weeks.

Then, in Father Flegge's most stern voice, he said, "No more *'Leave it to Beaver'* TV shows for the rest of the school year."

And that's how I learned, *"Cleanliness is truly next to Godliness."*

By-the-way . . .
We won the election.

SCHOOL DAZE

I remember the day I left home for college. Travel time was 6.5 hours by bus, some 300 plus miles away. At first, there was excitement in my brain believing all the possibilities of my future could now ring true. But as I sat down to eat my seven-course Italian sendoff lunch, reality set in.

I began to panic.

I had never been away from home before.

Maybe I should re-think this?

With a whine and a whimper, I struck the attitude of a 13-year-old girl getting her first pimple on the morning of the school dance.

My Mom wasn't having it. She pooh-poohed my anxiety by slapping down a picture of herself standing alone at *Ellis Island* with a hollow look in her eyes, wondering if she could get into America. I learned as she lectured me, half in Italian, half in English, that she was 8 years old at the time. Her family put her on a boat, a stranger to all, for a 6-week ride away from home. The black and white, crinkled around the edges, a bit faded photo was signed, *"Josephina Francis Casella, Ellis Island."* The June something, 19 something-something, date was faded.

And just like that, my *"woe is me"* mood was shut down.

There she stood, wearing an *Annie Hall* type hat, what looked to be an oversized man's overcoat, and a forced, half- baked smile. With only a briefcase for luggage, and a cardboard sign hanging around her neck with the acronym *"WOP,"* (without papers) scribbled on it, she had just traveled over the ocean by herself, not speaking the language, to escape war torn Italy. 4,283 miles away from her family in Italy, stood this little girl who would one day grow to be my Mom.

Now, she hovered over me as I grimaced about saying goodbye, fully experienced to be able to slap me in the face, *"CHER"* style, and command, *"Snap out of it!"* My Mom was in no mood for my 'Sad Sack' mood.

So . . . with a kiss and a hug, off I went to the bus stop, hearing my Mom's last marching orders ring out, "If you get in trouble, pray the police find you before I do!" It was a, *"leave the snivels, take the cannoli,"* summation for me.

With a gut full of a garlic laced lunch in my 'Nervous Nelly' stomach, I took the last available seat. It was me who had who had the 54 other passengers cursing the poor ventilation of a *Greyhound* bus.

Finally we arrived and I was officially a college Freshman.

What happened during the first 13 seconds of my first college class has run crystal clear and preserved in my mind forever. Here's the pre-amble to the humiliation.

Oddly enough, my first college class was *Psychology 101*.

Not *Economics*.
Not *American History*.
Nor, *Algebra*.
Nope . . . how apropos for my first class to be *Psychology 101?*

It was an eerie act of serendipity apparently designed to provide credibility to the mystery of why God is always on the side of the mother in any argument.

Here's how my #1 embarrassment rolled out.

I was the first to arrive at the classroom. I strategically picked my seat to be smack dab in the middle. Not front row, not back row, just as inconspicuous as I could be, dead center of the room. With only two minutes until the start of class, the now sold out room was just waiting for the teacher's arrival.

I was ready. I made sure of it. The final touches to begin my college life were complete as I memorized the teacher's name: *Professor Laidlaw.*

I remember being dumbfounded as all the other students were bantering back and forth, making quite a commotion; something never allowed during my last 12 years of school. Then the door swung open, the chatter and noise continued, and the teacher entered the classroom. I jumped to attention, standing with the posture of a *Buckingham Palace Guard*, and with the bravado of a rollercoaster scream, I barked out my warm welcome, *"GOOD MORNING PROFESSOR LAIDLAW!"*

The laughter from the class could not be silenced. Some kids were pounding the desk and gagging for air. Some threw pencils and erasers. There were a few spit wads as well. And the glare of revulsion from *Professor Laidlaw* gouged at my eyes. All that was needed to complete the scene was a bucket of pig's blood and the class pointing their fingers at me while chanting *"Carrie!"*

I was frozen. I couldn't move.

Amidst the sounds of the hecklers shouting, *"brown noser,"* and *"kiss ass,"* somebody yanked me by the arm back into my seat. As I sat, head down, with a claustrophobic mind, I swallowed hard and asked God, "Please don't let me cry, pee, or poop my pants."

I never looked up for the next 57 minutes, beating myself up for being so stupid not to have realized I had never been in a public school. Things were different here. How was I so oblivious to the obvious? I felt like an idiot.

All was resolved after class in the professor's office when I was summoned for a one on one admonishment. *Professor Laidlaw's* interrogation uncovered my history of 12 years of Catholic schooling. I blabbered out my alibi like a *Rudy Giuliani* excuse, stammering through most of it, with just the smallest hint of clarity woven in. But, to my surprise, at the end of it all, the gist of my message seeped through.

For 12 years, I, along with every other student, was *Stepford Wife* programmed by the *Nuns of The Holy Cross* to always stand and recite loudly a warm reception to all who entered. After thousands, if not millions of times saying, "GOOD MORNING SISTER MARY!", it became a knee jerk reaction I did without thought.

Professor Laidlaw whole heartedly laughed, too. He patted me on the back and said, "I should make you a case study for my Psychology Class. But don't do that anymore, it will turn out bad for you."

It was as if I had traveled to college by boat.

THE TASTE OF HABIT

(WHY I'M OVERWEIGHT)

The polite and politically correct way to identify an old age guy's annoying habits is to say, "He's old school." Old school has a redemptive and complimentary tone to it. My generation is not so polite. We, without hesitation, pretty much would just tell you flat out, "You are a pain in the ass."

I am not just old school. I am old school / catholic school. Old school is minuscule when compared to being old school / catholic school. Old school habits bring an immediate roll of the eyes by the younger generation. Old school / catholic school habits make the eye rollers want to go in the corner and throw up.

For twelve years, the Nuns, with God on their side, provided me a daily sermon on the values of repetition. I was taught to like the limits of routine, to find comfort in being in a rut, to stay on task. Give me the habits of a well-organized day and I am not only happy; I'll get to ride shotgun on the stagecoach to heaven.

You would think, I, more than anybody else, am better prepared to change my eating habits. But all that training in making something a habit is nowhere to be found when it is time for me to eat. When I diet, the tension between my mind and stomach increase. Then my weak willpower always convinces my full stomach to never send the message to my brain to quit eating.

Here's why . . .

At school, any complaints about lunch always ended with the Nun saying, "There are starving children in China." Only a woman wearing a paper picnic plate as a hat, can sell the value of *"waste not - want not"* under the guise of *"just one more bite."* Nothing cleaned my plate as well as guilt.

My eating habit *DNA* comes from being Italian. At home, every meal was a combination of celebration and debate. There was a lot of food with a lot of talk. Rumor has it that my parents invented the original dinner theater. We were expected to pipe up, chime in, make an argument, and comment about the topic at hand; and do it with a full plate of food, with a second and third helping on the way.

As soon as *"grace"* was said, everyone at the table looked like marionettes with the strings attached to the tail of a happy dog. It was a three act play just to pass the ketchup. What most people classify as a party, my family would call lunch.

Growing up, too much food never caused me any problems, because when I grew up, calories hadn't been invented yet. I rode a bike where I wanted to go, cut the grass with a push mower, and played three sports. The only time I sat down was to eat.

College was different. I found out the Italian way to eat was different from everyone else. I never thought it was when I was growing up. I thought everybody made a production out of mealtime. Little did I know, college food was bad and boring! My college eating habits were reduced to getting a gut full. Feeling full had veto power over taste.

For example: On weekends, the students in the athlete's dorm had to fend for themselves because the cafeteria was closed. With no money and growling stomachs, my roommate and I would eat dry *Quaker Oats*, wash it down with hot water to bloat our stomachs, run over to the library, and gaze at pictures of a roast beef dinner in the *Good Housekeeping* magazine, daydreaming that we just had just finished a delicious meal.

It worked! I swear we could smell the gravy! We tricked our brain and our stomachs every time.

Married life changed the game. There were remote controls, riding lawn mowers, a fridge and pantry full of food, and the best thing ever; someone else was doing the cooking. That's when I found out the word calorie actually has a definition.

So, for the past forty years, every once in a while, I will get a gut full of having a gut full, then try to diet. But most often my diet never lasted past the first battle between my brain and stomach. My stomach always wins!

The experts proclaim that for any diet to be a success, it must become habit.

My best old school /catholic school habit? Continually making a habit out of trying to eat healthy as a habit, then failing.

HACKY SACK

On occasion when my belt can be moved a notch to the left, remorse sits down next to me, crosses its legs and gives me a nudge making me think, I might owe the "*health gurus*" an apology. My belief that something's got to kill me, it might as well be what I eat, is wavering with every carrot I digest. I'm starting to grow accustom to feeling better about feeling better.

I have an embarrassing prejudice to get off my chest. I think vegetarians and vegans are odd balls. A quirky group of wayward misfits who ought to be felt sorry for. I give vegetarians and vegans a bum rap. I thought vegetarian was a girl thing, and vegan was some kind of motorcycle gang. Then my son became both.

I had never heard the word vegan before. At first, my wife and I wondered where we went wrong? Which parenting skills did we lack that motivated our son to walk away from the cheeses, sauces and meats of his Italian Grandmother?

Having a family member who is vegan has made me more aware of how populated this segment of society has become. It is like when I buy a new car. It seems the minute I have one, they are everywhere. Now that I am aware of such a thing, I run into vegans and vegetarians at every turn. My son's best friend is a vegan, which is surprising for how normal he is.

Shame on me for holding tight to my first stereotype of what a vegan is: a too mellow, too tattooed, too skinny, no energy, *Hacky Sack* playing, preachy, nose turned up, no fun, conspiracy theory, disconnected, pierced up poor soul.

OOPS!

As parents we feel lucky that both our kids escaped the long-term damage that comes from the normal temptations of adolescence. My kid's persuasion from the dark side was averted by continual threats and Catholic guilt. When that didn't work, I employed the tactics of my mother. Simply put, she would tell my brother and me in her broken English, "If you do anything wrong, pray the police get you first, because I'll kill you!"

With a rosary and a rolodex, I packed around the phone numbers to *Police Officers, FBI Agents, CIA Officials and the IRS,* just in case I got caught. Then, when the excuses ran out, I would shamelessly beg, "Just don't call my mom!" It worked. It kept me scared straight! Maybe there is something good to be said about that fear we all have of turning into our parents as we get older.

When I threw a big enough tantrum to keep our son out of the *Young Republicans*, I knew we were finally home free from all the bad influences that could scar him for life. Everything a parent worries about ended up cycling through its course, and now, as a young adult, we think our son is pretty much normal.

But NO meat! Where did that come from?

A diet with no meat and no dairy is a relatively new invention for Americans. For the youth of my generation, vegan had not been invented yet. If it had, it was a secret society type thing, hidden away from public view to avoid sympathy and ridicule.

I have a theory about eating meat, a simple conclusion that validates my urge to have a double cheeseburger for dinner tonight. Here it is: I think the jury is still out on the benefits of the vegan lifestyle. Every time I see the 100 + year old guest on the late night talk shows, you know the one, they are on TV for the sole reason of staying alive that long. That guest, male or female, always attributes their longevity of life to starting the day with a slab of bacon, three or four eggs, a shot of *Jack Daniels*, and a pinch of chewing tobacco to get them through to a whole milk, raw cheese, and dead animal lunch. Not once have I heard one of those century old guests proclaim, "I'm a cradle to grave vegan." The 100-year-old birth to death vegan is still in the making. I'll be dead before the verdict comes in.

I am surprised how many in my generation have converted to the vegetarian and vegan ways. But just like going to church, my age group signs up for what's good for us late in the game, hoping to make up for the past sins of bad eats and bad morals.

As I socialize with my son, and his no meat, no dairy friends, I find myself wide eyed and smiling as I interact with the clear thinking, reasonable, humble, agreeable, can take a joke, and younger than me generation. My typecast of the vegetarian and vegan crowd has changed.

I should eat something to celebrate. I'll treat myself to a cream-based bowl of clam chowder topped with bacon bits, a plate of salami and cheese, and some red meat for dessert. Or . . . I should repent with a true act of contrition by eating a vegetarian lunch and a vegan dinner while watching 4 hours of "*Hacky Sack*" on TV to see if they can get more than 3 consecutive kicks in a row.

I can't decide.

THE MARK MARINE COFFEE AND CIGAR DIET

I've never signed on for one of those fancy, structured, advertised weight loss programs. I don't think I need any of them. I have always believed that my stubborn ass nature could summon the necessary will power to start a diet on command. But no such luck! Any time I dropped a noticeable amount of weight, it was happenstance. On the occasion when I weighed less today than yesterday, I promptly backtracked, double checking yesterday's menu, hoping to find my own fountain of skinny.

Here are my results.

My best weight loss diet is:

-   *"The Mark Marine Coffee and Cigar Diet."* This is a theory-based diet. The hypothesis is based on the premise that there are no calories in either black coffee or cigars with the added benefit that the thick release of smoke from the cigar would fumigate and kill any air born germs. I could lose weight and never catch a cold.

My second-best weight loss diet was forced upon me by a lady in a robe.

-   *"The Deposition Diet."* This is a nervous breakdown-based diet. I was the star witness in a legal matter, my faculties were all confused.

I didn't eat right, sleep right, or poop right. A stenographer, 35 lawyers, and a contest for billable hours stole my appetite and nerved me up to the point of burning calories in my sleep.

My best tasting diet comes from my uncanny ability to ignore the facts and deduce a conclusion because, it makes sense to me!

- *"The Deep-Fried Diet."* This is a defensive based diet. In an effort to combat salmonella, E.coli, trichinosis, worms and mad cow disease; I say, "Throw it in the deep fryer." No bacteria can survive 10,000 degrees. I never lost much weight, nevertheless, I never got bacteria-based diarrhea.

As you can tell, I'm a theory guy. It's all about the attitude. Plato and Aristotle make sense to me. *MENSA* candidates do not. Story problems I can handle, it's the unpolluted mathematics and science that baffles me every time.

The moral of the story, weight loss by theory, not science, equals being 20 pounds overweight for life.

LUCKY ME

By accident I caught a full view of my lower backside in the reflection of the medicine cabinet mirror when it swung open. The angle was perfect. What I saw was not. I have a *Sex and the City* butt. Not that good, hard body, *Chip and Dale* butt. My butt is the, "doesn't look too bad with clothes on, just don't take off the underwear," butt.

Remember that episode of *Sex in the City* where Samantha starts to fall for that "older fellow" who, for the entire 30 minutes, looked the part, dressed the part, talked the part, and just stepped off the cover of a *GQ* magazine only to be written out of the script after Samantha caught a glimpse of his droopy derriere when he went to pee? Except for the look, dress, talk and *GQ* part, that could be me. I was hoping the poopie diaper look for a butt would wait until I was at least 65.

My friends who eat nutritional and healthy food are telling me to exercise. Come to find out, being busy all day burns minimal calories and does nothing for toning the butt muscles. Apparently, because of my age, (old), being busy isn't good enough. I must compensate for the grey hair with calisthenics. They say that *Jumping Jacks, Sit Ups,* and something called *"Pilates"* goes hand in hand with a good healthy diet and firming up a deflated bottom.

I don't understand. I thought the purpose of exercise is to get a free ticket to the chow down & overeat buffet. The reason I need to diet is because I don't exercise. If I was exercising, I wouldn't need a diet, I'd need a gift certificate to the *Chuck-a-Rama* all you can eat buffet.

I always thought exercise and diet to be an either- or proposition. For me, exercise is a mental punishment, a torture. The physical part of exercise is not the problem, the boring part is. I have never exercised for exercise sake. For me to exert myself, exercise must be a biproduct of the activity I'm doing. Game preparation is easy exercise for me. Exercise of its own accord is retribution. *Sit ups, Push-Ups, Jumping Jacks* and aerobics might as well be a water drip torture test. And I thought *Pilates* was plural for the bad guy in *Jesus Christ Superstar.*

Jogging seems to be everybody's answer to my "*What should I do for exercise*" question. Jogging seems to be the holy grail of mindless exercise. Everyone wants me to jog. In college I tried jogging for exercise when my girlfriend dumped me for a return missionary. The further I ran, the uglier she got. A blind date and a couple of pickup basketball games later, I put the *Nikes* back on the top shelf where they belong.

I ran a marathon once, and it was easy for me to train for the race. The 26-mile, 385-yard distance had the two requirements needed to motivate me. A finish line and 1800 people trying to do it better than me.

A race I can do. A jog in the park I can't.

The most noncompetitive running I have ever done was inspired by romance. I wanted to impress a girl, (now my wife), by running to the ends of the earth to see her. Or in this case, 7 miles to her house. The younger generations will have a difficult time understanding this, but believe me, back in my day, when I was your age, it took quite a bit more effort for a guy to get "*lucky!*"

Here was my plan: Each night around 11:00 P.M., just as Paula's swing shift as a nurse ended, I would lace up my sneakers and run to her house for what I assumed to be a one-way trip. Everything was in place to play the sympathy card and win a sleepover.

I had two fail safe "*let me stay the night*" lines. One was, "*I need a shower.*" And the other, "*It's so late, the trip home on foot would be unsafe.*" I was sure the girl of my dreams, from the kindness in her heart, would offer me the couch. Then, with no *PJ's* and a sleep walking alibi, I could blame the overnight events on the serendipity of the moment. No such luck! But I got in great shape trying to get "*lucky.*"

At my age things have changed. No one wants to compete. And worse yet, young people will let old people win so no one gets hurt.

So, the dilemma continues. Find the motivation to jog and exercise without the motivation of a scorecard or the encouragement of *Cupid's* arrow. Or, keep the *Sex in the City* butt, drive over to *Home Depot*, and remodel the bathroom with no mirrors.

BUT MY THUMB

Everyone needs a diversion when melancholy sets in, something to take your mind off your perception that the world is out to get you. What's your diversion? Eat? Drink? Sex? *Rock & Roll?*

When I'm down and out, I look to the comfort food for my reprieve. And there is so much to choose from when your Italian.

But have you noticed? Skinny people's comfort food is shopping. Instead of reaching for a bag of corn chips, they grab the credit card with the highest limit.

When I have a bad day, I want lasagna, endless bread sticks, and a trip to *Baskin-Robbins*. The light weights head to the Mall.

Thanks to my effort to lose a few pounds, my pants are too loose. Another inch in the loose direction and someone is going to give me a skateboard.

DAMN! I have to go shopping! I hate shopping!

Here's the problem: No matter the store, be it grocery, department, or specialty store, all the people I see with a vest and a name tag, came to work that day, specifically NOT to man the cash register. If you have an emergency, don't try to check out, 15 of the 16 checks stands never have anyone there. And the twelve employees within arm's length, mingling as if they were waiting to catch a bus, are incapable of helping you because they swore at orientation never to enter the promised land of cash registers. Your only option is checkstand 16, operated by someone moving like an extra in a *Jacques Cousteau* underwater frogman film, reacting so slow and deliberate, you are seconds away from transforming into *Jack Nicholson's* ax scene in *"The Shinning."*

Shopping for clothes is my worst! And buying pants is my nightmare.

I would have made a good cave man. I liked the way the men dressed, and the woman didn't. Take a couple of fig leaves for some underwear, the animal skin from last night's dinner for a shirt, a half dead raccoon for a hat, and every *Neanderthal* would be all dressed up with everywhere to go.

But I confess. When I shop for clothes, the problem is as much my fault as it is theirs. I get embarrassed trying on pants. It's not my size or indecision that is the problem, it's my shape. For one specific reason, my body has never been in proportion. I have an odd shape.

Here's how that happened.

Right out of college, chasing my dream job, each day I would run up every single step of every section in a 40,000-seat baseball stadium. I soon became known as *"Thunder Thighs."* I had a six-pack stomach, a 30-inch waist, and here's the carnival freak show measurement, I had 34-inch thighs. Each thigh was bigger than my waist. Finding a pair of pants that fit was torture!

When I could afford it, I would buy a pair of pants with a 42-inch waist to fit over my thighs, then head straight to the seamstress to "*take them in,*" reducing the size to 30 inches to fit my waist. The reconstructed pants looked OK, but now my front pockets were where my bum pockets were supposed to be, and the bum pockets were on the cutting room floor. Every time I reached for my keys, I put my thumb in my butt.

Consequently, I have never owned a pair of *Levi's*. *Levi's* are not seamstress friendly when it comes to alterations. When I asked, "Could you take these in please?" I always got that tilted head, eyes wide open, mouth shut tight, look a beagle gives you when he is thinking, WTF?

When I was in shape, denim never fit my thighs. When I am not in shape, my gut overhang was fashion inappropriate. But now that my thighs have toned down a bit, and I can damn near fake it with my belly, it's off to the Mall!

I set out to find myself a pair of *Levi's*. I shopped at three different stores. It didn't go well. There were too many questions to be answered. What style? What color? What leg? I couldn't pass the verbal examine being administered by the clerks. *Levi* could have its own category on *Jeopardy*. Who knew?

After an afternoon of dejection, dazed and confused by trying to solve my fashion *Rubik's Cube*, I hugged the mannequin wearing *Dockers*, and then of course, I robotically wandered into the food court. I was off the wagon and ready to eat. I had a plan. Pizza, burgers, fries and *Mrs. Fields*. Just the diversion I needed.

As my mouth watered in anticipation, I didn't even make it past the first cash register. I had no way to pay. I couldn't get my thumb out of my butt! And no one was there.

GOD'S LOL

God laughed out loud when he invented taste. Taste is God's joke on the other senses. My other 4 senses are independent and have a built-in response to unwanted stimulus. If I don't want to see something, I shut my eyes. I can tune you out when I don't want to listen. And I'll plug my nose if you pass wind. Even my sense of feel can be controlled by an ibuprofen and a, "*I should have known better.*" Only my sense of taste calls for an immediate board meeting. My taste is by committee. All five senses get into the act.

Whether it be,

- the crisp sound of the sizzling bacon,
- the mouthwatering smell of freshly baked bread,
- the eye pleasing sight of a *Food Channel* cake,
- or the *Fred Flintstone* macho feel of breaking off a whole turkey leg; my other senses are an aphrodisiac for my taste buds.

All this conflict is caused by taste. Taste is comfort food's foreplay. And when the dust settles, the better the taste, the more the comfort.

In years past, I would find myself bewildered when my mother, a fashion queen from downtown Manhattan, would respond to my style of dress by saying, "Your taste is all in your mouth!" Having given it some thought, all I can say is, "No kidding."

My desire to be comfortable never goes away. I suspect you are the same as me. I toss and turn to get cozy in bed, jostle in the theater seat to feel just right, and change clothes as many times as it takes to find the right fit for the day. Being uncomfortable makes me antsy, being antsy makes me hungry. When I am unable to relax, I eat something. I go on the hunt for *"comfort food."*

It is an English language snafu that the word comfort is used in the same phrase with the food that can kill you. It is peculiar and ironic that this eating binge thing is called *"comfort food."* But the definition of *"comfort food"* fits me. Nothing calms my restlessness like a grazing trip through the kitchen. If there's no kitchen, just point me towards the *Twinkie* isle.

Experts tell me everything I like to eat for fun, everything on my *"comfort food"* list, can jump start the end of life. For me, a bucket of broccoli just can't cut into the satisfaction required to smother my yearning for a tasty, comfortable, food treat. Show me the *"junk food!"*

It's a psychological addiction for me, a malfunction in my mind. When the urge hits, I tie mental yellow ribbons all over my mouth waiting for the tasty treats to come home. *Tofu* dished up under the guise of *"comfort food"* is a regret and disappointment. It's like showing up to a blind date only to realize your dinner companion looks like an older version of your already old mom. The lipstick can't hide the truth. I know myself all too well, one course in and I would look for a graceful way out. Or in the case of *tofu*, find a bag of double stuffed *Oreos*.

My problem with *"comfort food"* is now clear. I am half-ass backwards on my approach to solving the problem. I will continue an attempt to eliminate the cravings for *"junk food."* I will make a steadfast effort to orchestrate the ebbs, flows and whims of my other 4 senses and to prevent the inevitable surrender to the demands of the committee. I know it will be a losing cause. I'll never learn it's the appetite, not the food that makes eating a delight.

BREAKING BREAD

Too many times I come close, but no cigar. I hate the almosts of life, not finishing the task at hand, leaving loose ends dangling, postponing the inevitable, only to be haunted by a plethora of *would of, could of, and should of,* regrets. Even in the simplest of goals, not busting through the finish line turns me into a sour puss. For me, an all but achieved goal is like kissing your sister, just a nice gesture.

For the last few weeks I was hoping to proclaim that my weight had dropped to less than 200 pounds. I thought it would be a nice surprise. A WOW moment. Something to brag about. When I started to watch my weight a few months back, my weight was 220 pounds. As in all the other times, I expected this particular effort to be just another good try on my part, eventually ending in diet defeat. But every time I stepped on the scale with the needle pushing to the left of 220, I got greedy; I wanted more of the less.

Now 18 pounds lighter, breaking the number 200 has turned into a quest. I get close to 199; I can see it, I can smell it, I can feel it, and every time I eat something that tastes like crap but is good for me, I can taste it. But the tease continues, and it can be depressing.

I dropped the first 18 pounds as if my metabolism was orchestrated by a maestro; a perfect rhythm and sequence resulting in the subtraction of weight that I hardly even noticed it happening. Then, out of nowhere, when I reached 202, a U turn, it went the other way. Not much, just a pound or two more. The next day, another U turn, a couple of pounds less. It has been that way for two weeks. I have fluctuated between 202 pounds and 205 pounds. Back and forth, back and forth. I am doing a diet *Cha-Cha-Cha*.

It's a curse! The diet gods are taunting me for telling one too many vegan jokes.

When the scale reads 202, I do an end zone touchdown dance on the bathroom floor, high five the towel rack, and blurt out a sequence of *Matthew McConaughey's*, "All right, All right, All right" in anticipation of a number less than 200 showing up at tomorrow's weigh in. When the number reads 205, I re-adjust my stance, change my posture, and quickly look over each shoulder to see who sabotaged my weight with their toe on the scale. Every weight in between is a "what done it" mystery. I am hooked on being unhooked from 220.

For two weeks I have pretended it was no big deal, but now I am nervous with that feeling of, "Here we go again." I don't want to be one of those people who diet that people come to pity and say, "That's too bad . . . he gained it all back."

So far, my research for resolving this problem is to pout about it. Sometimes I like to pout. But when I got back to my typical, annoying, pain in the butt, non-pouting self, I took a poll. I asked my wife, my kids, my friends, and everyone else healthier than me why I am in this 2-week weight loss teeter-totter.

After hearing the facts of the case, their unanimous conclusion is, "It's the BREAD!"

I LOVE BREAD! It's my Achilles's Heel of dieting.

Everything about my food consumption for the day is just where it ought to be for me to keep losing weight, except for the bread. I thought bread was a freebie; a zero points utilization of getting something for nothing. I don't butter it, I don't jam it, I don't cinnamon and sugar it. I eat it raw and naked. Awhile back I heard white bread is a waste of the chew and swallow needed to get it into the digestive system. No problem for me, I switched to that road base, *Mar's* surface, sandpaper replacement bread. Just what I thought the doctor ordered to justify eating a basket full. But no, when it comes to losing weight, bread is bread. I want bread to be the mulligan for my diet. Healthy people say I will stay in diet purgatory if I don't ban the bread.

The Bible says man cannot live on bread alone, but my diet would work a lot better if the manna from heaven would have been tofu.

SHUT UP AND EAT!

Because of a nice gesture in the form of a gift, I just received a box of health food bars. Receiving gift wrapped health food is a first for me. I usually get something that is bad for me. A box of cigars, a fifth of something, or a basket full of salami and cheese. Healthy for me or not, I like getting surprises for my mouth.

When I was in grade school, gifts of food came in the form of *"Hot Lunch Day."*

"Hot Lunch Day" was always a gift, despite the fact it only cost 25 cents. *"Hot Lunch Day"* didn't happen very often, but when it did, the whole tone of the school day took on the joy found in the anticipation of a Christmas morning.

You see, there was no cafeteria at my Catholic elementary school. We didn't even have a lunchroom. On my normal school day, I would sit in the same chair, at the same desk, where I sweated bullets for the first 3 hours of each day praying, *"Sister Corporal Punishment,"* (hit your knuckles with her ruler), didn't call on me. Lunch time, even at my desk, was something I looked forward to. As long as I sat up straight, took small bites, and chewed with my mouth closed, all was well. If not, *"Sister"* would appear out of thin air and spread Catholic guilt all over my *Fritos.*

With a paper napkin as a place mat, I took in the smell of surrounding bologna sandwiches, peanut butter and jelly, and a few whiffs of the kid's lunches who were lucky enough to get last night's leftovers for their lunch that day.

I loved leftover meatloaf sandwich days. I would always scan the room trying to make a trade deal. If only I could get rid of the apple that my mom insisted was a dessert for a *Hostess Cupcake* or a *Twinkie* for my after-lunch treat. My negotiations always failed. The other kids would look at me funny, shake their heads, and give me the look of, "Are you kidding me?"

My normal daily lunch routine was eating for need. "*Hot Lunch Day*" was eating for fun, prompting the saying of "grace," to be said twice as loud.

Sometimes it was *Sloppy Joes*. Sometimes it was Chili. Sometimes it was my favorite, Hot Dogs. The best news! Every "*Hot Lunch*" always included a homemade cookie. And no apples for dessert.

Even if it wasn't tasty food, no-one knew any better, because picky eating was considered to be taboo, something connected by the Nuns to be a direct insult to Jesus himself. Simply put, in Catholic School lingo, it was a, "*Shut up . . . Eat . . . And be happy about it,*" commandment.

The same rules applied at home. Who amongst us didn't hear growing up, "You'll eat what I made, or don't eat?"

But we never had "*Hot Lunch Day*" on Fridays. For Catholics, Friday was no meat, eat fish day. In order to get into heaven, there was NO meat allowed on Fridays. Commanded by God, or in this case, the Nuns, which in our minds, were the very same thing. We were policed into believing even a thought about meat on any given Friday would lead us into a life of sin.

Some kids got peanut butter and jelly. A few others ate cheese sandwiches. But us kids with moms from the old country always got tuna fish, because . . .well, Jesus and His fish was a thing.

Catholic school lunch on a Friday smelled like Pier 39 because most classmates brought their mom's unique version of a tuna fish sandwich for lunch. It was the worst kind of stink. So, every Friday we all became comedians, thinking we were funny, coming up with our very own "*Dad Jokes*," 20 years ahead of schedule.

-     What is the difference between a guitar and a fish?
★   You can tune a guitar, but you cannot tuna fish.

Or, how about this one?

-     Did you hear about the evil tuna?
★   He was rotten to the albacore.

Oh how we thought we were hilarious!

But, when we got into Catholic High School, "Friday Fish Jokes" got more befouled in their humor.

- What did Stevie Wonder say when he walked down the wharf?
★ (Well, I hope you know the answer, because I'll be sleeping on the couch if I print the punch line.)

Consequently, I'm not a big fan of fish.

Four decades later, during a trip to South Korea, I damn near turned away a gift of food, but instead, sealed the deal for my distaste for all things breathing water.

Here's what happened.

After giving my speech to members of *The National Assembly of the Republic of Korea*, I was invited to be the guest of honor at a dinner hosted by the *Prime Minister of Korea: The Right Honorable, Lee Han-dong*, in his private dining room.

I was out of my league! There I was, rubbing shoulders with the *Prime Minister of Korea,* his *Minister of Defense, Minister of Education, Minister of Justice,* and the *Korean Speaker of the House.* This was a BIG deal for me. Yet, strange as it sounds, of all the thoughts I could have had, right at that very moment, with so much jitteriness washing over my being, my mind decides to think about my college girl friend who dumped me for an architect. "Boy, I wish she could see me now!" I thought.
(but that's another story)

Being comfortable while you eat a meal the traditional Korean style, which is sitting butt flat on the floor, is a tough deal for Americans. No chairs are there! Korean's have "*innie*" stomachs, and Americans, (me), have an "*outie*" stomach. When I sit on the floor to eat, my belly button covers my belt buckle, I can't breathe, and the size of my thighs prevents me sitting at the table like everyone else in Asia; crossed legged, Indian style.

And crap, there's no forks!

The dining room was spectacular! Beautiful in a dramatic and eye-catching way. Picture a dining table the size of a regulation pool table without legs, sitting flush to the floor, made entirely of inlaid pearl, that they tell me is over 1,200 years old.

Being the honored guest, custom has it, I was to be presented first, with what everybody at the table unanimously considered to be a most special, Korean food delicacy. And, Korean dinning protocol calls for me to take the first bite to start the meal, giving all others the green light to dig in and start eating.

Wow! What Korean culinary delight could it be?
Kimchi? (fermented vegetables)
Bulgogi? (marinated beef barbecue)
Soju? (a clear, colorless distilled
    beverage of Korean origin, 53%
    alcohol by volume.)

Dressed in a full length Korean traditional dress called a *hanbok*, a 20 something beautiful woman, face powdered bright white to look like a porcelain doll, enters the room, moving like a ghost whose feet never touches the ground, and glides towards me carrying a tray with a bowl filled full to the top with a gift of food just for me.

She bows, kneels down beside me, and with the smile of a cherub, puts the tray and bowl on the table right in front of me.

O my God! It's a bowl full of baby octopuses! And their ALIVE!

Everything I had ever put in my mouth up to this point in my life has been dead. I've never eaten food that changed direction right in front of my eyes. These things were squirming, fighting, and wiggling all over the bowl. With the arm stroke of Vanna White, Korea's version of a "*Geisha Girl*" proceeds to chop stick feed me a heaping portion of creepy, crawling, ALIVE, baby octopuses!

Just as I was summoning the courage not to act panicked, the *Prime Minister*, along with all who were in the room, started to applaud, grinning ear to ear, as if to congratulate themselves for being the perfect hosts.

Then, with all eyes on me, these creepy crawly sea creatures fought their imminent death by attaching themselves with their suction cup tentacles to the inside of my cheeks. With my reflexes responding in an urgent need to regurgitate my mouthful back into the bowl, I used the only option available. Kill! By FAST, CHEW, CHOMPING!

I bit down fast and hard into the sensation of cracking vertebrae and the squishing out of whatever is in the inside of a baby octopus.

"Please God don't let me hurl!" I prayed.

With a forced smile on my face, you know that look, a cross between a shit eating grin, and the wincing of the eyes during a "*Charlie Horse*" muscle spasm in your butt, I choked it all down, gave two thumbs up to the group, then pulled off a look of fake gratitude to adorn my face.

"*Sister Corporal Punishment*" and my Mom would be proud!

And it wasn't even a Friday.

DEJA VU ALL OVER AGAIN

PLAN "B"

I daydream too much. But I like it!

I have two types of daydreams. One type is a controlled event where I become the director of my trance. For example, my favorite forced daydream is musing about how I will spend my *Powerball* winnings.

A close second is all those times, just like every other little boy in America, I would play pretend in the backyard of my house on *Hillsdale Drive*. There I stood, baseball bat in hand, where I was simultaneously the radio play by play announcer and cleanup hitter for the Yankees. As I stepped up to home plate, (one of my mom's everyday acrylic platters turned upside down), with bat in hand, I acted out my call:

"Mark Marine steps in the box.
    It's the bottom of the 9th.
    Bases loaded.
    Yankees down 5 to 2.
    2 out . . . full count.
    There's the pitch, a breaking ball!
    Number 7 swings.
    There it goes.
    Going, going, GONE!
    Yankees win! Yankees win!
    The YANKEES WIN!!!

(It was always against the *Red Sox*)
God, I love that daydream!

Then there is my other kind of daydream. It's never planned. It sneaks into my brain via stealth mode, takes control, and for not long enough, my mind just drifts away. One minute I am in real time, the next, I'm off dreaming of things that happened in my yesterdays. I'm there and not here. Prompted by a smell in the air, or sound to the ear, or the view of nothing important, I transform my being to another place and time.

These are the moments in my life where I am mentally transported into a thick coated bubble, alone in a thought, so removed from the present tense that people around me always ask, "Are you alright?" But when it happens . . . GOODBYE! I am mentally absent from the time being. No matter the surroundings, there I am oblivious, hypnotized into a black hole of recollection.

Those around me can tell I'm in a faraway zone by that glazed look in my eyes. To grab my attention, my name must be repeated several times with a snap of the fingers, each time a little louder, to bring me back to the present tense. Mark . . . Mark . . . MARK!!!

With a few blinks and a head shake, my mental *DeLorean* screeches back to the present tense with these words from whoever was barking my name, "Where the Hell were you just now?"

So when this happens to you, where does your mind go?

More often than not, my mind flashes back to decisions, that if made differently, might very well changed my present station in life. It's my own version of "*Sliding Doors.*" In 1998 there was a movie called "*Sliding Doors.*" A classic "*what if / what could have been*" scenario film.

When Helen (*Gwyneth Paltrow*), a London ad executive, is fired from her job and rushes out to catch a train, two scenarios take place. In one, she gets on the train and comes home to find her boyfriend, Gerry (*John Lynch*), in bed with another woman. In the second, she misses the train and arrives after the woman has left. In the first scenario, Helen dumps Gerry, finds a new man and gradually improves her life. In the second, she becomes suspicious of Gerry's fidelity and grows miserable. Each scenario was life changing.

Here's my "*Sliding Door*" moment that prompted this story.

I was minding my own business. I just started the first leg of my morning routine; poop, shower and shave. Out of nowhere, I wasn't here! I was there! Gone back to September 2, 1960. It was the day for me to start "*all-day kindergarten.*"

Everybody was happy. I was happy because finally, I wouldn't be stuck all day, every day, having my Mom as the sheriff. And my Mom was happy because, well . . . she wouldn't be stuck all day, every day, being the sheriff.

I was supposed to enroll at the same school my 5th grade brother was attending, *St. Ann's*. For my parent's convenience, it would be the same bus ride, same time schedule, and most important, same Catholic guilt built into the curriculum. All happening with my 6-year older brother now wearing the sheriff's badge.

There were tears in my Mom's eyes when the priest proclaimed there was no room in the *St. Ann's Kindergarten Inn*. The kindergarten class was jam packed full.

I remember being mouth droppingly stunned to witness, for the first and only time in my mom's life, she was speechless, and had to accept NO for an answer. My Mom could, and would, make a New York argument with anybody and everybody; but Nuns and Priests were off limits. I couldn't enroll at *St. Ann's!*

An impromptu *"Plan B"* developed before my eyes. A lady wearing a rosary the size of a towing chain with airplane wings for a hat, *Sister Mary*, suggested another school across town called *Bishop Glass*.

For a minute my mom was elated, after all, a Nun is a Nun, who are all equipped, in full regalia, with a, *"God is on our side,"* arsenal of Catholic protocol.

But, oh NO!

After being at *Bishop Glass* for less than 2 minutes, a jolt to our "*Plan B.*" Lo and behold! With a planet of nearly a billion and a half Catholics, there wasn't enough 5-year-old Catholics in this small Mormon bedroom community to fill a kindergarten class at *Bishop Glass*.

Until the day my mom passed, what happened next was her "*go to*" living proof that prayers can be simultaneously answered in real time. Standing there in dead silence, with desperation painted on my Mom's face, Father Sloan, a *Bing Crosby* type priest, said in his heavy Irish accent; "Good Lord, put him in first grade and pray no one will know the difference!"

For all the times I thought my mom was truly happy, this time seem to have eliminated any need for a future bucket list, as it was to be her greatest moment of joy.

So off I started, 5 years, one day old, and a first grader, a year too young for the norm: the runt of the school litter.

At first, I didn't know any better. I didn't know I was the runt. Then, a couple of grades in, I noticed the other kids had two more candles than me on their birthday cakes. And when I stayed a tenor and the other boys moved to the other side of the choir two years sooner than me, and the boys on the team were getting hair in places I wasn't, I started to figure it out.

I remember casual friends, as well as my family members at our yearly family reunion, when introduced, assumed I was ahead in school because of my smarts; something easily dismissed upon observation. And I was saved the embarrassment of having my Dad be the chauffeur for my *Senior Prom* by some Italian connections and using my Uncle's Boise, Idaho address to get a driver's license ahead of schedule.

Sixty-three years later, and points along the way, another favorite daydream has been born.

Now I embrace the difference the implementation of *"Plan B"* has made in my life. There are no regrets in this daydream. And not in the bubble of a glazed over eye, but rather, in crystal clear thinking. I now celebrate the fact that I was acting my age all those times I picked the #1 most stupid thing to say or do off the asinine leader board.

It's Déjà Vu all over again.

BUY A CLUE

I own up to the fact that sometimes, not very often, I find enjoyment in the exercise of being crotchety. Can you be happy about being unhappy? Do you enjoy a good mad? I can! And I do!

It is an odd feeling to find myself being content with a bad mood. But when I hunker down into the makings of a lousy day, I am soothed by the awkward serenity.

When I am on one, a really good one, nothing frustrates me more than some, *Pollyanna*, happy all the time, *do-good-er*, bringing a can of happy to my misfortune. When it's time for me to cry in my beer, I want to drink alone.

It's the small stuff that puts me down in the dumps. I get melancholy about why so many people don't have a clue. I can take in stride the unplanned and unsettling tragedies of life. A house burning down, a job lost to a backstabbing boss, a heartbreaking early death of a loved one; all seem to be by design, placed there, just because it's part of the deal of being alive. I figure the BIG disappointments are written into the contract of life, something we all signed on for when we pulled the rip cord to get out of the birth canal. But leave the cap off the toothpaste, and outcome the *"F" bombs*. The grimace look on my face leaves stretch marks on my cheeks and neck.

It's the little things, those little details that can be controlled, not being controlled, that brings out my frowny face. I conclude that with just a smidgen of observance, a clueless wonder could just pay attention the least little bit and make the world a better place. Yet there is daily proof that the majority of people don't have a clue that there is a majority of people.

The list of little things that wreck my day is long, but at the top of my list of the *"Have No Clue Club"* is something that I think is near the top of your list too.

Driving too slow in the left lane!

All of you have experienced it. Being stuck behind, with cars stacked up in the rear-view mirror, that ever present, holier than thou, *"I'm going to heaven and you're not,"* pain in the butt, driving 55 miles an hour in the diamond lane during the morning commute.

It's a self-serving belief that allows the slow poke to justify having blinders on to the world around him. And if you can make eye contact as you rattle snake your way to pass on the right, you will certainly see the look from that pleasant, hands at 2 and 10, happy to be alive, no stress face, exclaiming, *"Jesus loves me, I can be oblivious!"*

A quick Google search shows no evidence that God, His Son, or the Holy Ghost endorses not having a clue as a saving grace.

I've been to 63 years of Sunday Mass and not one homily was ever given saying, "Go forth with your head up your butt." In fact, I'm pretty sure the Bible says it's a sin if you are oblivious. And if you're Catholic like me, it's a *Mortal Sin*. You are going to Hell!

But don't worry, stay to the left, the line will be moving really slow and the stacked-up people behind you will finally be grateful.

BITE MY TONGUE

I have two oral issues.

First, I swear too much! My favorite time to swear is when an inanimate object is getting the best of me. Grabbing the wrong wrench for the wrong bolt quickly gets ratified with an expletive. And when I'm in charge of the *IKEA* instructions, a full-fledged seminar of cursing occurs with no break for lunch. Sometimes I feel bad about feeling so good after an obscene filled tirade, but swearing at something not alive is therapeutic for me. I imagine it to be equivalent to a spa day for a woman scorned.

My next oral issues is, I think I'm funny when I'm NOT!

My mother noticed my smarty-pants attitude at a young age, usually right after I talked back, warning me that my smart mouth would come back to haunt me. She was right! When my mind is idle and aimlessly free, I regurgitate past conversations, always worrying if I said the wrong thing, at the wrong time, wishing for a verbal do-over.

My fall from grace happens when I not only want to, but truly enjoy, being a "*shit*" at the wrong time, for the wrong reason! Nothing feels as good as a snappy comeback when someone should have minded their own business in the first place. I love that touché moment when a wise guy gets put in his place. Even if the wise guy is me.

Here's how it rolls:

Each time the urge to be sarcastic moves near launch mode, an inner battle of my good and bad angels takes place. Good angels encourage patience. Appearing only when needed, there the good angels sit, perched on my collar bone, cheer-leading in a quiet voice to take a step back, breathe deep, and don't be a jerk!

On the other shoulder, the bad angels camp out, taking advantage of a spiritual *Homestead Act,* invented by God, to secure property right next to my inner ear for a *Beetlejuice* type community, welcoming me with a megaphone, tempting me to drop a *"F" bomb* and dawn my next move wearing an ass hat.

I'll say something I shouldn't have, blurting out a smart aleck remark, then immediately catch a glimpse of the bad angels in my peripheral vision high fiving each other, grinning ear to ear, sporting the thumbs up salute, elated that their temptation took me down once again.

But there's one specific time I was a wisenheimer that still haunts me to this very day.

I remember when my son came home from his first day of school in the small town we just moved to and said, with a touch of melancholy in his voice: "Dad, my teacher said you don't love Jesus because you drink coffee!" My bad angels kicked into formation like a college marching band, and without a hem or a haw, I exclaimed, "Tell your teacher your Dad says he hopes her legs grow together!"

I thought then, and still do think now, ha-ha! Touché! Good for me! But I confess, *PTA* meetings seemed a touch awkward after that.

I feel bad about that day, but just a tiny bit. I want to tell you that it didn't come out the way I wanted it to, but no, at the time, it came out just as it should have.

My bad angels win even in remorse.

PRETTY BOY

Sometimes the one line, off the cuff words people say to me, stay with me for life. Not the phrases we all know, like some biblical passage, or a line from an inspirational *John Kennedy* speech. No, what I'm talking about are those tuning fork, crystal clear, perfectly timed comments that cut sharp and deep, leaving their mark like a seared cattle brand.

Don't we all have our own versions of *"You had me at hello."* Or, *"You can't handle the truth?!"*

I do!

My wife, way back 40 plus years ago, while we were convincing ourselves we were meant for each other, right in the middle of one of our original *"lover's spats,"* shut down my rant and rave by loudly interrupting me, saying . . . "You ever notice, Mark? You're never as mad as when your wrong."

Damn, I hate having my bluff called.

When I get angry because I'm right, well, that's therapy for my soul; I talk like an accountant. Magnified mad means I'm guilty, and I turn into *R. Kelly* answering a *Gayle King* question.

So, I have a couple of questions here. One . . . Don't you keep a little more *"mad"* stored in the tank just for when you are wrong? And . . . Why is it my wife never gets mad?

Back to the one-liners.

There was this time before I got married, when a quick, 3-word quip, spoken by a college cutie, who I was convinced I could make like me, changed how I looked at myself, (literally), for over a decade.

There we were, driving along, sitting side by side, two love birds, so happy because Chevy hadn't invented cup holders or a console yet, and the front bench seat with the gear shift on the column was still a thing. Driving with one hand on the wheel and one hand on her knee, I would be forgiven if God forbid, I had to stop short, and my hand happened to shift a little up her leg. There was plenty of room to not need plenty of room.

In a split second of time, I took a quick glimpse of myself in the rear-view mirror. You know how one does, just a quick double take, to see what she sees. And before my eyes got back to the road, interrupting *Hey Jude* on the radio, my date says with a touch of disgust in her voice: "YOU'RE SO VAIN!"

I was embarrassed and humiliated and quickly turned off the radio just in case a *Carol King* song was next.

I didn't look into another mirror with someone else in the room until 15 years later when this happened; I was turned down for a career making job because of the way I look.

From the neck down I was in good physical shape. In fact, probably the best condition of my entire life. Still showing the remnants of playing ball, I was at 3% body fat and I felt like a *Greek Warrior*. But I wasn't "Nice enough looking in my face." - so said the producer.

Out of 800 applicants, I was a finalist to be the co-anchor for a top-rated TV magazine show. Not getting the job demoralized and disheartened me because of the reason why.

The producer liked my style, and he liked my way. He even liked my voice, which I know has never been FM quality. The deal killer was my head and face. He explained:

"You are too rough looking!"
"Too bushy of eyebrows!"
"Too curly of hair!"
"Too gruff of a face!"

He continued on: "Our audience needs a more, well . . .more pleasant looking fellow. Sorry Mark, you look like you just got off the *banana boat*. We need a *Terry Wood / Randall Carlisle* looking type of guy."

Terry Wood and Randall Carlisle were the pretty boy local news anchors at the time. And by the way, the guy that got the job looked like Terry and Randall had a kid.

I was crushed! It kicked my butt!

For 2 weeks after, I wore a baseball cap and a pair of *'nylons'* on my head while sleeping, praying I would wake up with straight hair. I bought a Sherlock Holmes 5X magnifying glass and precision tweezers to tackle my eyebrows. And I thought with a blessing of practical magic, a *"KEN"* doll under my pillow would smooth my face out by osmosis. It was a, *"Mirror, mirror on the wall, why can't I look like the other guy, once and for all,"* moment. I wish I had that pretty boy look. Crisp, clean and sharp.

My parents looked like movie stars, with cut and chiseled features so noticeable, that strangers would ask for an autograph and a photo, because even though they weren't famous, they looked the part. My grandparents on both sides, not so much. Lucky me, I inherited my appearance gene from my grandparents.

My next of kin originates from two distinct and separate regions in Italy. One area produced *Sophia Loren, Mona Lisa, and Fabio.* The other – *Yogi Berra, Jimmy Durante,* and women with mustaches. The *Sophia* and *Fabio* chromosomes skipped my generation.

I'm not a bad looking guy, but I would have to actually accomplish something for someone to want my signature on a napkin.

Now, at my age, (old), being self-absorbed about being a pretty boy has been reduced to a haircut. And not that fancy of a haircut at that. I have been *"flo-bee-d"* a time or two and walked away with a happy spring in my step.

And look at the one liner that just jumped into my brain, spoken by my Dad.

"A kick in the butt is still a step forward!"

YES, I HAVE NO BANANAS

I have proof women invented *Fake News*. In fact, women are so good at this one particular bit of *Fake News*, I will bite the hook, line, and sinker of the *Fake News* excuse a woman provides to tap dance around the *Fake News* they just told me moments ago.

This treasured ability to spin this one specific untruth into being true, is human genome magic; only to be found in a girl. And before I make my case, let me say, God bless them for it.

Here's the story:

Women can say they are "*in the mood,*" participate like they are "*in the mood,*" and most important, portray the ecstasy of crossing the finish line "*in the mood;*" but we men will never know. Only the female knows. Because odds are, according to the sex gurus, somewhere along the line, all of the before mentioned compliments we men so often believe are true, are in fact, *Fake News*.

None of us males think our woman *fake it*. For we are all macho manly men. We figure a female *faking it* just happens to the other misfortunate guys, who are not like us, believing in our own hyper masculine minds, that our bedroom partner thinks we are *Dwayne "The Rock" Johnson* in disguise.

But for me, secretly hidden behind the *Casanova* file in my brain is that *Billy Crystal / Meg Ryan* restaurant scene in the movie show, *When Harry Met Sally*. In the scene, Harry and Sally are sitting at a restaurant getting ready to eat their lunch. He has pastrami, she has turkey. An argument about sex starts up just as Sally takes apart her sandwich and puts it back together again in the way she prefers. Harry starts boasting he is certain the women he sleeps with have a good, and most important, satisfying time. But Sally wonders if perhaps the women were *faking it*. Harry's jaw drops like he has a front row seat at a *Yo-Yo Ma* concert, then scoffs at the possibility of any woman he had ever been with "*faked it*." Just as Harry's smirk is about to reach its pinnacle, Sally proceeds to show him what a fake orgasm looks like, and how it is indistinguishable from the real thing. Probably one of the funniest movie scenes ever.

That scene lurks in my mind, ready to haunt me every time I think I've reached bedroom superiority, causing me to proclaim out loud, just like the lady sitting at the table next to Sally, "I'll have what she's eating."

And that's the catch. Every woman since Eve was born with the acumen to pull off "*faking it*." And every man since Adam can't. Even when I'm in the mood, roaring to go, there's no "*faking it*." When what should be is a frozen, spicy, *Italian Sausage*, but in reality, is an overcooked *Ramen Noodle*, the look on my face is that of a child who just opened a Christmas present to find socks and underwear.

What a disappointment!

Shouldn't equal rights demand there be an outward physical sign for women equivalent to a boner? How about an eye twitch, an uncontrolled lip flap, or inflated ear lobe? Something for God's sake! There should be an unequivocal and noticeable, uniquely designed, physical response in the female body that declares to her partner, "LET'S DO IT!"

Why can't men *"fake it?"* It's not fair! When Eve got the rib, she also stole man's ability to *"fake it"* in the bedroom. Men can say they are done and satisfied, but the lack of messy evidence will always prove them to be a liar. Not so for females. We men got nothing to go by. We must take them at their word, hoping it all wasn't an act.

Of all the things that suck about getting old, having to pee when I don't want to, and not being able to saddle up when I want to, tops the list. When I was young, I could hold a pee like a racehorse, and best of all, my lap rocket was always on *DEFCON 1*.

In those good old days, I was like every other teenage boy, who would have to use a *Pee Chee Folder* to cover that part of the anatomy that had a mind of its own, sporting an unsponsored *woody*, sticking out like the *Circus Circus Casino Clown* billboard saying, "Go ahead everybody, make fun of me," all while being scared to death some smart-ass progressive girl would screech out for all to hear, "Hey Mark! Is that a banana in your pocket or are you just happy to see me?"

Now, 45 years later, the least little sound of running water will make me have to pee. And worse, I must take a pill, concentrate like a *Zen Master*, and hope to God that if everything is working the way it is supposed to, the moment won't be killed by the thought, "What if she's *faking it*?"

If a *Q and A* session is allowed at the *Pearly Gates*, my first question to God will be, "How did you get this so backwards?" After all, we were all taught, you are in fact, a GUY!

I worry God will be a bit chapped, that with of all the frustrations He so cleverly wrote into His creation of humanity, this is the one question I couldn't wait to ask.

But just think, if He only would have switched places on these old person physical algorithms, there would be no waking up every 2 hours to tinkle, and better yet, even at 65 years old, just a quick glimpse of a *Victoria Secret* commercial would open the blood flow flood gates.

What was God thinking?

Now in my mid 60's, I conclude one of two things happen when *Cupid's* arrow hits below my belt and I am in "*the mood*"and all is well, because. . . it ended well. Either, I really am that good! Or, my wife's kind and gentle soul, took one for the team, not wanting to burst my bubble, and "*faked it*."

I'll never know. Because, how-be-it women invented *Fake News*, men initiated the original, *"DON'T ASK, DON'T TELL POLICY."* I don't ask, and she don't tell.

My romantic life is good. I foolishly go to bed brainwashed healthy and happy, so sweetly do I sleep, as if my wife has never *faked it* at all. I have been a *"Stud Muffin"* for the last 42 years.

My very own *"FAKE NEWS!"*

MOTHER TERESA MOTORS

Every time I get a bit uppity and start thinking I am all that, and a bag of chips, my resume' grabs the stick shift attached to my attitude, and with no clutch, grinds me back to neutral. Thirty-four times I got hired. More times than that, I didn't. At the time, I wasn't sure if my next move was working my way up the ladder, or down. One thing is certain, I can't get off the damn ladder.

Here's the list of the times I heard "you're hired," not so much to be read, but to quantify it's laughable length.

In chronological order...
- car wash boy
- flower delivery
- silk screen operator
- milked cows
- diesel fuel jockey
- bread baker
- baseball player
- bellman
- truck driver
- car guy
- back to car wash boy
- newspaper circulation manager
- short series newspaper writer
- seasonal newspaper columnist
- sportscast TV host
- Burger King manager

- night club manager
- limousine driver
- 7-11 graveyard shift
- Coca-Cola merchandiser
- morning show talk show host
- ski instructor
- janitor
- back to car guy
- invented car finance program
- owned a dealership
- syndicated talk show host
- newspaper boy
- author
- office in Seoul, Korea
- erosion control specialist
- honorary Chaebol Chairman
- 6 international patents
- storage unit manager

What an embarrassment! When asked for a resume', my face flushes red, I become speechless, then, using a *Regan in Exorcist* head spinning technique, I look for a rock to crawl under. When it happens, I feel like I was shot at and missed, and shit at and hit; standing there only to explain why my resume' looks like a phone book.

I envy those of you that have accomplished a one and done career. I wish I was you. You, content in doing your thing so well, day after day, year in, year out, can now stand there, with the world at your feet, satisfied in a job well done.

Not me! Just like a dog off leash at a fire hydrant trade show, I marked my territory with just enough me, then move on, smelling out the next opportunity to bury my bone.

You would think I would be a seasoned pro in a job interview. But NO! I suck at it!

Here's my worst and best interview depending on which side of the desk you were sitting. A job I never really wanted yet ended up being an employment defining career. To prepare: I got a haircut, was early to bed, ate non flatulence making food, bought a new suit, and asked God to wish me luck.

When I entered the owner's office, there sat the main man, the cream of the crop of the *car guy* industry. Bigger than life, he rocked back and forth in a, *"I'm the boss, you're not,"* oversized, leather, executive chair. He was sitting behind a desk, that if seen in a stand–alone picture, would be mistaken for the workstation of a Supreme Court Judge.

What caught me off guard was the landscape of my interview setting. There, six non-matching folding chairs were organized into a half circle facing the boss, with a single chair in the middle. Picture it from a bird's eye view, looking down and seeing a mini half-court basketball floor. The 3-point line would be the six chairs, the pole holding the backboard would be the famous boss, and the chair for me was right smack dab in the middle on the foul line. Now, condense the picture down to a too close for comfort size, and you can see what I saw, and understand my first thought; "Good Hell! This is a prayer circle. And I'm the sinner!"

Immediately the interrogation began. As I stood up to answer the first question, the owner points directly at the chair and says, "No, no, no - please stay seated." Now what? With my back facing four of the six people, I begin to wonder how in the world could I properly face who I am talking to and answer their question?

Rather than ignore the direct command of the person holding the future of my employment in the palms of his hands, or rudely trying to speak *Jim Carey* style, bent over, choreographing the words through the crack in my butt, I opted to transform my feet into a *dance clogger*.

While sitting with my butt firmly stuck to the seat of the chair, I grabbed the underside of the frame, lifted the chair with my butt stuck to the seat, and with the posture of *The Hunchback of Notre Dame*, I tapped danced myself, with the attached chair, now part of my ass, around to face whomever was asking the question.

Question after question, there I was, doing a concocted isometric exercise, clumsily shuffling my way, making 180 degree turns, fighting the chair and my body, trying to face the one I was speaking to. I had to bite my lower lip to prevent myself from laughing out loud at the fact that everybody there, except me, thought this was OK.

About 30 minutes in, out of breath and with achy arm muscles, I sensed the finish line was just a swivel or two away. Then this happened. The 5-foot 4- inch high automotive consultant jumps up on his tippy toes, ballets himself to within an inch of me, and screams down from his man-made perch; "WHAT MOTIVATES YOU?"

With the look on my face of a 9-month-old baby trying to figure out what coochy-coo means, I stated what I thought to be the obvious . . . "To do a good job."

"NO! NO!, NO! That's not it," shouted the consultant, now prancing around the half circle with his hands on his hips, shaking his head. "THINK!" He screamed. "WHAT MOTIVATES YOU?"

As panic started knocking on my door, I scrambled to find the right answer. "I want to be a valued employee," I said. "Be a good husband and father. I want to . . ."

"WRONG! WRONG! WRONG!" Yells the *General Patton* want-to-be, now pacing flat footed back and forth. "C'mon. . . "THINK!" He commanded.

"Pride?" I asked. "WRONG!" He shrieked. "How about success?" I whimpered. "NOPE!" He barked. "Working on a team?" I feebly guessed. "Give me a break," he said with disgust.

Whatever I came up with, the answer each time got louder and louder and was always the same. Wrong! Wrong!! Wrong!!! WRONG!!!!!!!

I'm lost! I have no clue. I got nothin.

Then, this jumps off my lips in my most sarcastic voice; "Why don't you tell me what I am supposed to say, and I'll tell you if I thought it?"

"MONEY!", he screeches. Money absolutely must be what motivates you! You gotta want to make the big bucks! You've got to love money!"

With a chuckle I asked, "Well, you are going to pay me, aren't you? This isn't Mother Teresa Motor's is it?"

I thought that was funny, but the silence in the room said otherwise. No words were spoken, no uncomfortable coughs, the consultant even stopped his stomping around the half circle. I could tell they all were waiting for my amendment.

The eerie quite caused me to mentally flashback to the day I left for my first *Spring Training* of an upcoming baseball season that has now long passed. There stood the ghost of my Dad as if he were the only one in the room. "Mark," he said. "Always play the game like you don't need the money. The things that matter most can never be at the mercy of the things that matter least."

"I ain't getting this job," I thought to myself. So, I piped-up and hopped up onto my soap box.

"Look," I said, "You read my resume'. You saw I played baseball back in the day. Not once did I say, I'll play better, I'll hit *better*, I'll pitch better, if you just move me up a level and pay me more money. I always believed that the money would take care of itself once the verdict was in about my value. I don't get it! I ain't your guy!"

Orchestrated by the consultant breaking the silence with his parade of my horribles, the noise and commotion was back. What was supposed to be an employment interview meeting, now resembled a hastily planned press conference. Everybody was yelling questions at the same time.

"Screw this," I thought, shaking my head with my eyes closed while tilting my head towards the floor. "I'm outta here." It was time to leave.

Just as I reached the door to exit, I hear above the brouhaha, BOOM! The owner, sitting behind his fancy oak executive desk, stopped rocking in his fancy executive leather chair, and slammed his open palm down on his desk and said, "Hire him, I'm going golfing."

And that's how I got that job.

HISSY FIT

I can throw a fit when needed can you? Not that involuntary knee jerk reaction tantrum. Instead, that hissy fit exaggeration of anger to make the point kind of outburst. It's a parental teaching skill learned the hard way from generation to generation. Although both a mom and a dad will subscribe, it is the father's ability to blow a gasket at the right time, for the right reason, that will make us shudder long after they have passed.

My mother's outrage could be predicted. I always knew I crossed the line before I crossed the line. Because my Dad was a calm guy, so much so, even my friends thought of him to be "*cool*," his ability to upheave the moment would leave me stunned with disbelieve that I was anywhere near the line that should not be crossed.

My fits aren't that effective. As my wife points out, "Good Hell, Mark! How can anybody tell when you're NOT exaggerating?"

Now before we move on here, let me say that my wife, and the people that know me, over exaggerate my propensity to over exaggerate. So, there!

My Dad was different. There are two types of Italian dads. There are the Italian dads who are a mini me of their mother, but with a penis. Then there are the Italian dads who are *Vito Corleone*. My Dad was a "*DON*." His exaggerated anger was very effective. When what I am about to tell you happened, I didn't recognize whether or not it was intentionally aggrandized by my father, but I remember that Sunday night in 1965, 55 years ago, as if it happened last night.

There our family sat, watching Sunday night TV. A weekly ritual we adhered to after enjoying a dinner of two different pastas, pizza, 3 kinds of salads, endless garlic bread, and homemade cannoli with fresh fruit for dessert.

My Mom was stretched out on the couch, my Dad relaxed in his *Lazy Boy* recliner, and me and my brother were on the floor, just far enough away from the TV not to block the view.

This was a very special Sunday evening of TV watching for my Mom, brother and me because we were about to watch our first, brand new, COLOR TV! My Dad, not so much! A new color TV was not that big of deal for him. His usual after dinner routine, whether the TV was color or black and white, was to hunker down in his chair, read the *Sunday Salt Lake Tribune* newspaper, with the TV only there for background noise. It was a *Norman Rockwell* painting. That is . . . until this happened.

I wanted to watch *Disney* with the *NBC Peacock* opening its feathers and the *Disney Castle* fireworks introduction. My Mom insisted on *Ed Sullivan* because more likely than not, she probably had met that night's performers from her younger days growing up in New

York. And my older brother, just to be a shit, thought it to be fun to argue for anything but.

Here's how we argued. The three of us became human channel changers! This was pre remote control days. To change the channel, you had to:
-   get up,
-   go to the TV,
-   form your hand into a vise-grip,
-   have the wrist strength of a diesel mechanic, then be prepared for that grinding, gear stripping sound the small hubcap channel changing knob made every time you turned it.

With voices raised, arms a wailing, and shuffling like a bunch of *Roller Derby Queens*, we fought to change the channel to our favorite show, one forearm shiver at a time. Then from behind the newspaper came my Dad's booming voice: "Stop it! You'll break the TV!" As if the house referee blew the time out whistle, we went silent. But just for a second. Then it started again, and now, it was a competition between three people, who could not stand to lose.

It was louder and more passionate in the second round. The three of us had worked ourselves into a bit of a frenzy. But oddly enough, amongst the in-house mini riot, what I remember most, was that distinct gear grinding noise of the channel changing piercing above the clatter.

Then it happened! My Dad, not saying a word, calmly put his newspaper down, took 2 steps with a "*Bend it like*

Beckham" crow hop, and BOOM!!! KICKED THE TV SCREEN IN! He sat back down to relax, picked up the paper, opened it, and said in a monotone voice; "Buy your own TV to break."

Nobody dared say a word. Even my *3 act play* mother was silent. But in that moment of quietude, I swear I caught my Dad so slightly tip the newspaper and give my Mom a wink and a nod.

Exaggerated Anger. That was my first lesson. What was yours?

PET PEEVES

Pet Peeves. Like you, I have a few. Those little things that gnaw on my mood, so much so, it can wreck my day. Some vexations are familiar to all of us; bad customer service, disgusting restaurant kitchens, someone without a clue. But most pet peeves are like dental records, unique to the person being annoyed.

One of my most simple pet peeves is, well . . . simple. The things that bother me, don't bother you! I want the things that irk and bug me, to irk and bug you too!

I always feel like I'm smack dab in the middle of an "*I Love Lucy*" re-run when I start to lose my head while those around me keep theirs; concluding that the levelheaded ones just don't grasp the gravity of the situation. Which leads me to another one of my pet peeves, a daily aggravation settled into my psyche for the sole purpose of frustrating me at every turn. That is, why doesn't everyone think like me? After all, each of our mothers made it clear, the whole world thinks like them. I figure it should be hereditary.

Here's one of my pet peeves that makes my skin crawl, giving me the *Heebie-Jeebies*. Walking barefoot in public places. Not on a sandy beach or neighborhood pool kind of thing. No, it's the strolling over, and on top of, dog pee, cowboy chew spit, spilled soft drinks, car oil leaks, and who knows what?

Let me give you the *Heebie-Jeebies.* Picture in your mind walking barefoot into the men's bathroom of a biker bar saloon, where the aim is never bulls eyed, and you know your toes are not feeling water. That's what I think when I see bare feet strolling through the city streets. See what I mean? Unless you are an *Andaman Islander,* put some damn shoes on! *Heidi Klum* could show up at my front door with nothing on but the radio, and if she got there walking barefoot, I would switch my allegiance to celibacy.

I have a couple of pet peeves that involve God, which makes me nervous. I keep these frustrations hidden away in the footlocker of my mind, tucked away to avoid a first-class ticket on the train to purgatory, a place where Catholics get a chance to explain what the Hell they were thinking at the time.

First: "*Yay Jesus*" piano music at Mass! Mass needs organ music in a *Gregorian Chant* language no one really understands. Leave the piano playing, hand clapping, high fiving, praise the Lord singing, to the professionals, the Baptists. I've been to their services. The music fits. It works!

I feel blessed at every Baptist's gathering I've been to, feeling as if God commanded the right music, for the right church, at the right time. And . . . they are better at it than us. Besides, I'm sure there is a spiritual patent infringement when Catholics try to pull it off.

Then, there is this pet peeve which I really struggle with, because it sounds terrible to say out loud. *PRAYER!*

Today's billboard versions of prayer makes me feel like a lobbyist, always asking for something. I cringe at the thought that God has become equivalent to an *Aladdin's Lamp*.

The common phrase used is . . . Pray for _____! (fill in the blank) Really? Is prayer supposed to be an effort by humanity to convince our personal version of deity that He should prove to us, He likes us best, by granting our wishes?

For example: When leaders say something to the tune of; *"Let us pray for the war to end."* Does God really sit there with His angelic board of directors and a score card to proclaim: *"Damn, so close! Just three Our Father's and a Hail Mary short! Let more people die! The war continues!"* Do we really think God works that way?

When the outcome is favorable to the one doing the praying, I hear people recite, *"Our prayers have been answered!"* But without fail, my mind immediately goes to a place showing a vivid, heartbreaking, harrowing picture of someone who prayed more and got less.

Don't get me wrong, I think prayer is a good thing, but the reasons why we pray suck.

I'm not any good at this modern-day prayer phenomenon, thank God!

(now that's a prayer)

ME AND MY BRIGHT IDEAS

"You and your bright ideas!" I hear that often. And always with a dose of sarcasm. It's a *Pavlovian* response from those who know me, and have come to expect, my mind perpetually provokes me to act out what is in my brain.

Bright ideas started at a young age with me. My first bright idea brought a quick retort from my Italian, Catholic, wooden spoon wielding mother. A high brow eye roll and head shake; her generation's version of WTF???

When I was four years old, the first bright idea that I remember was a to my surprise, not my best. An inflatable dart board! Didn't think that one through. Later on during my single digit years, my bright ideas either got me into trouble, or became a necessity to get me out of trouble.

Here's one that I thought was clever, which sounded good at the time, but got me grounded for life, even beyond my mother's grave . The punishment of *"bathroom duty"* was enforced for, well. . . EVER! And to this day, 56 years later, my wife has never cleaned a toilet since the *"I do's."*

I was 8 years old. There I was, just like you this morning, lying in bed, trying to figure how to blow off the day and play hooky. I, at the time, had a gut full of school. I couldn't take another day of the Nun's child development catch phrases that they implemented for my generation.

All day long, everyday it was: "*Snap to it, Chop-chop, Spring in your step, and don't camp out,*" -- which were always followed by: "*Sit up straight, No slouching, Put that away,*" and of course, "*IMPROVE YOUR PENMANSHIP!*"

All the above, according to the "*Sisters,*" were God's commands to make me a better person.

Not today I prayed. "Please Lord, let me miss school!" My prayers were answered. Here is how I connected the dots.

My Dad, who always left for work earlier than needed, before anyone else was awake, kept his custom that morning and indeed left the house in plenty of time for me to spring into action.

Out of nowhere, the right side of my brain kicked into action, ignored the obvious consequences, and masterminded the idea of moving the hour arm of every clock in the house ahead one hour. It would be my own personal "*School Fatigue Saving Time!*" Five years later, President Lyndon Johnson stole my idea and invented *Daylight-Saving Time,* something I feel pretty good about to this day.

My inner *Einstein* deduced that because my Mom, who, until the day she died, stayed a *Manhattan Subway* gal, having no desire to learn to drive in the foreign city of Salt Lake, would be handcuffed from a satisfactory solution if I missed the school bus. I knew if I missed the bus, the time restraints of coordinating transportation would be in my favor and *VOILA*, I would be home for the day!

I *'almost'* got away with it! I remember the exact moment when *'almost'* burst in, and I was busted!

It was at 9:30 a.m. that morning. Here's how it went down.

At 9:30 a.m. Mountain Standard Time, the TV show "*Queen for a Day*" was not on. It was supposed to be on. Rather, *Romper Room* was on. *Romper Room* was a children's show that usually was on the TV about the time I was scheduled each day to brush my teeth, grab my lunch box, and scurry to the bus stop.

Of the many things my Mom was, being organized, structured, and systematic was her personality anthem. Each and every weekday she would schedule her day to be uninterrupted while she paid homage to that day's chosen royal commoner. Perplexed, confused, and disoriented because "*Queen for a Day*" was not on as expected, my Mom, with her brain wheels visibly racing, noticeable through the look in her eyes, started re-checking all the clocks in the house.

Kitchen clock ✓
Grandfather clock ✓
Alarm clock ✓
Wristwatch ✓

Just as I was mentally patting myself on the back for pulling this one off, my Mom springs out of her bedroom in a military march with a death grip on my Dad's "*dress up*" pocket watch.

Oh, oh!

I remember the look on her face when the light came on above her head exposing my guilt. There was no eye roll, there was no head shake. But the wooden spoon was released from my mom's apron's holster with a, "They gave me the wrong baby at the hospital!" and a, "Wait till your Dad gets home!"

Thus, I have got toilet cleaning down pat.

In college, most of my clever contemplations were for fun. How about . . . *the "Air Enema?"* How great would it be to have influenced flatulence upon command? Grab a *Bic Lighter* and you would have "*blue darters*" at will. Every college kid would be elated! Back then it made sense to me. And now that I think about it, it still makes sense to me.

Later in life I was sure my brilliance would bring me big money. A few of my bright ideas actually made a bit of a living for me and my family, albeit, we never did acquire today's standard of what we all consider rich. I am convinced though that my best million-dollar ideas, which never did get their money legs beneath them, are still out there waiting for someone just like you to be the next *Bill Gates*.

Maybe one of these:

Mark's Back Scratch Shops! No back rubs, no hot rocks, no cucumbers on closed eyes. Just two hands, ten fingers and straight French cut nails! Ahhhh!

OR . . . My 40-year-old sidelined aspiration, sitting poised, waiting like a caged rescue dog, stewing patiently for someone to call it their own.

"DIAL A DOUGHNUT!"

I figure it works for pizza, why not doughnuts? I love how the name rolls off the tongue, and the logo is perfect! A delicious sprinkle doughnut used as the face of a phone dial, a smiley face for the hole, 0 to 9 numbers correctly spaced, with a bright orange receiver placed on top. A bright idea even a 10-year-old would grasp.

As I shared my enthusiasm for having enthusiasm with my 11-year-old granddaughter, she morphed into the ghost of her Great Grandma, standing there perplexed, confused, and disoriented. Papa she said, "How do you dial a phone?"

Damn! "Scroll, Swipe and Tap a Doughnut" just doesn't have the same ring to it.

Time to grab the Ajax and find a toilet!

MAKING THE GRADE

People like me annoy the shit out of people like me!

Here's the story.

I love surprise visits by old friends. Nothing changes the tone of the day like reminiscing about the past. Even people I don't like, given enough time gone by, make for an enjoyable visit. When asked, "How's it going?" – I will tell you . . . every detail, of every story . . . twice, just to make sure you got it.

My old friend Jim stopped by this afternoon just as I finished my chores out on the property. After a few minutes of happy reminiscing, right in the middle of being lost in our let's remember session, Jim I suspect, in order to veto hearing the same story again, blurted out, "I miss your '*Type A*' personality!"

At first, I thought, "Good for me! I like getting *A's*!" I was never good at getting them. I can't remember the last '*A*' I got. I think it was a memory class.

Back in my day, grading on the curve was the latest, greatest way to brand your schoolwork. Being surrounded in high school and in college by a gaggle of '*A*' getters, I never got another vowel on my report card. So, I was feeling pretty good about myself getting an '*A*' for my persona.

But then I Googled it. *"TYPE 'A' PERSONALITY."*

WHOA! REALLY??? This is me? I feel like I owe the world an apology!

Not to go *Wayne Dyer* on you, but this deserves a longer look in the mirror, a touch of soul searching.

Here's what I see you're seeing.

Arm length friends, at first blush, say I am wound to tight! But I will gnaw, scratch, kick and scream to show you what a tranquil guy I am. I consider myself a patient man and deem it to be just a shame the people around me never notice it. If the people around me would move a little faster, they would see how calm I can be.

The everyday people in my life are eager to proclaim I don't prioritize my frustrations like the rest of the world. They say I'm backwards, an anomaly. They say, for me, BIG problems equals NO problem! That I can keep a *Texas Hold'em Poker face* amidst the chaotic commotion of a true tragedy. But block the grocery store produce isle because it's time to tell your neighbor about *Little Johnny's* science fair project and out comes *F...*#&@%^£, son of ....!*

It's these quirky characteristics of my personality that wears down the people around me. According to their straw poll, I was being sent to a different planet, there was an eclipse, and I landed on earth by mistake.

Realizing I might be a *Type 'A'* personality brings out the *Type 'A'* personality in me. The pendulum of my character continually swings side to side. I am never in a mental pause, stationary in my emotions. And I'm convinced this hyper disposition is a good trait because I am confident that I can always summon the proper response at the proper time. Unlike others, I don't think it to be a negative to bounce from having an obsession for things to be in order, to never leaving well enough alone. It seems normal to me to feel the happiest when everything is in its place, yet, status quo makes me anxious. And I admit, I would rather drive in the wrong direction to keep moving, than stay stuck in traffic pointing the right way.

It's the little comforts in my life that make me happy. Yet, my personal constitution states that whatever formula is prescribed for success, I say double or triple it, just to make sure. No matter what the venue, I believe overkill is the answer. However, without hesitation, I make fun of the extremists. I am a zealot about not being one.

This therapeutic exercise of looking within has turned my soul searching into a room full of *Fun House* mirrors, distorting my perceptions as I search for the good in being such a pain in the ass. At every angle I look, there's a deformed reflection exposing my *Type 'A'* personality characteristics, making me sad that the reflection I am seeing is way too familiar.

Later that same day, finally, a reprieve; a welcomed phone call from my son; something to do with an old garden tool in the shed. Certainly, this conversation will validate all this *Type 'A'* personality stuff is not as bad as it sounds. Dismissing his landscaping questions, I asked, "Describe my personality?"

His monotonic answer could be an ear worm in a *Clint Eastwood* movie. "Well Dad, you can be a bit anal at times!"

ANAL???!

Good grief! Anybody got a Wayne Dyer greatest hits box set for sale?

MAN'S HAPPIEST MOMENTS

"Man's happiest moments is when something is leaving his body." Pause . . . think this through. Yep, I pretty much nailed it!

Fart, sneeze, pee, poop, orgasm, even clearing the throat for a good old fashioned logy, when what's in a man's body heads toward the exits, in that nanoscale moment, nothing else matters, all is good in a man's world.

Albeit the moment is fleeting, right then, right there, you are one happy guy! And with lottery winning luck, if a man can sneeze, fart, and have an orgasm in harmony, well, . . . GAME OVER!

To prove my point, especially for the women out there, ask the man in your life, not the question, "What makes you happy?" – knowing full well the scripted answer passed down from the wisdom of our fathers and grandfathers will be, "Why of course, you honey, you make me happy!"

No, in this case, leading the witness is not only appropriate, but mandatory.

Uncut, unrefined, simply ask the man in your life, "Are you happiest when something is leaving your body?" Then prepare for a large, beautiful, blossoming bouquet of roses and a compress hug saying thank you for paying attention!

Just as happy, are the times men discover the untethered joy in the activity leading up to, or following behind, the actual event of emission. For example: What little boy hasn't had a pee sword fight? With the giggles of happiness, and amazed in the wonderment of no toys needed, we all became "*ZORO*," not giving a care that the bathroom floor now looks like a *Rain-X* windshield wiper commercial.

How is it that a woman will politely blow her nose so softly that a stethoscope could barely hear it, while a man uses a stuffy nose as an excuse to become a rodeo air horn? Or better yet, men will just pick the booger for that therapeutic moment of bliss, rolling it into a ball, and flicking it.

And always battling for first place on the fun discharge bucket list, is what woman call a toot, and men call, *"good job buddy!"*

With a whew and a grin, we guys observe, through sound and smell, the joy in the release of a held in fart. Whether it be an outboard motor sounding, *let er rip*, attention grabbing fart. Or the legendary *SBD*, (*silent but deadly*) fart. The equal opportunity for a well-timed and satisfying "*pull my index finger*" trick for the kids and grandkids is ever present.

Woman pass wind and apologize. Men bust a gut, high five whoever is near, fan the smell to surrounding noses, then drop to one knee, and pound the floor in laughter.

Men are elated when something leaves their body, because, just like an appendicitis operation, the alternative sucks!

Whether it be fighting back a sneeze, or tap dancing while grabbing your crotch to hold a pee, or changing from briefs to boxers because the family jewels look like the navy-blue *New York Yankee logo*; euphoria is in the release!

One time I my pooped my pants in public! I was 45 years old. At a restaurant no less, where nonfood stink has no camouflage. I was not there with family and friends, people who on the best of days would give me at least a sympathetic benefit of the doubt. NO, lucky me, it was a business breakfast, jam packed with people, whom except for my co-host, I didn't like, but selfishly needed in order to make a living.

Dressed in my *John Gotti* pinstripe power suit, with a noticeable, but not too flashy tie, and the, *"I'm a cool guy"* tassel shoes, I found that when the omelet was off my plate and in my stomach, my gut felt like a can of *Silly String* with the shoot button stuck down. And it sounded that way too! I had to POOP! How embarrassing. I couldn't hold it any longer!

With the politeness of *Fred Rogers,* I excused myself and high stepped it to the men's room.

Cursed by the gods of clean underwear, the one stall bathroom was occupied with a newspaper reading cowboy enjoying his *"happy moment"* with no intention of speeding things up on behalf of a cheek squeezing city boy.

The guy could stand flat footed and shit in a belly dumper, I wasn't even going to ask.

Just as I was negotiating in my mind the mechanics of using the urinal or the sink as an outhouse, or even try sneaking into the women's room, BAM! IT WAS TOO LATE!!! My mind was tardy in its deliberation. The verdict was in. It felt squishy, smelt terrible, and looked like a bowl of meat lovers chili dropped to the bathroom floor using my pant legs as directional guides. The *John Gotti* pinstripes we're no more, blended away with a butt full of embarrassment.

What to do???

It seems my ability to critically think turns to shit when I shit. Yet, at this pinnacle of humiliation, with discomposure running wild over the fabric of my persona, secretly, at that moment of liberation, that $1/100^{th}$ of a second, right before the panic of reality came rushing in, the pre-amble to the male constitution was born . . .

"Man's happiest moments is when something is leaving his body!"

A LEG UP

Italians don't give a one or two sentence answer. Nope! We need to tell a story. That's why it takes us 3 hours to eat.

Unsolicited, something you just said, prompts me to connect some dots that no one knew were there, and without a pause, turn my answer into a modern-day parable. It's the unintended consequences of being raised Italian. Why answer with a simple yes or no when the overkill of a dissertation could seize the moment?

We *'WOPS'* are so convinced you want to hear what we have to say, it never dawns on us there might be a retort to our pontificating. Except for me. I've been told too many times; *"You're full of shit!"*

Makes me feel sorry for my wife. For the last 43 years, my wife has been the presiding officer over calling out my *"B.S."* Without a word, or even a look, and with no emotion, she emits an aura that travels like a mist, fogging up my perspective, letting me know that, *"I'm full of shit."* Or for her, the *"PG"* rated version . . . *"You're Out in Left Field."*

Being *"Out in Left Field"* is not a compliment. It is a polite, non-Italian way to say, *"bah-fungoo!"* (Go stick it in your ass!) The term *"out in left field"* came to mean you're crazy and *"full of it"* because of the fans of the *New York Yankees* and the *Chicago Cubs*.

Here's that story.

The *Chicago Cubs* first location, which is now the *University of Illinois at Chicago College of Medicine,* had a mental institution behind left field. The fans in the left field bleachers could hear the mental patients wailing in anguish and moaning in agony throughout the duration of every game. The fans in the *Left Field Bleachers* were surrounded by lifelong, season ticket holders from *"One Flew Over the Cuckoo's Nest."* Baseball fans throughout the country thought the *Chicago Cub Left Field Bleacher fans* were as crazy, and as *"full of it,"* as the patients sequestered behind them.

Over *in New York*, the term *"Out in left field,"* was meant to describe people who were unknowing, or unhinged enough to buy a ticket in the *Left Field Bleachers* for a much different reason.

In the 1920s, when *Babe Ruth* was in his prime, anybody sitting in the left field bleachers were looked at as silly. *Ruth*, being a power hitting left-handed batter, predominantly hit most of his home runs to right field. So those sitting in the left field bleachers were much less likely to catch a home run ball because they were sitting in the wrong part of the stadium. You were considered to be *"full of shit"* to pay money to watch a game from the seats out in Left Field. Consequently, being in New York, if you sat out in the left field bleachers, you as a Yankee fan, could expect to be booed by your very own home team fans.

Back to me being full of it . . .

Because I tell stories like it's a filibuster, you might think I was born and bred out in *Left Field*, prodding you to respond, just like my wife, *"Mark, you're full of shit!"*

But I contest!

Aside from:
- my Facebook posts that are way too long.
- saying hello with a greeting that is longer than a hobo's lunch hour.
- expressing goodbyes that need an intermission.
- and only finishing my soliloquy when the planets are aligned, and there is a northerly flow from the Alaskan peninsula.

I pretty much get straight to the point.

Here's the one and only time I was happy to be told I was *"Full of shit."*

There I laid, flat on my back in the hospital. I was lost in thought wondering if taking a 98 mile an hour fastball in the elbow of my pitching arm was a career ending injury. All those tests, x-rays, and blood work were just a fact gathering exercise to determine whether or not I was worth the money. I was a human lab rat.

Because there was no life ending prognosis, and the stark realization that I was a guinea pig for the baseball trade deadline, I became a model patient. I took my own food tray back to the cart, changed my own bed, and never hit the nurse call button for anything. That is, until the head nurse, doing her, *"coming on shift"* midnight rounds, walked in wearing the mandatory nurse's uniform, which by today's standard would be a sexy *Victoria Secret Halloween costume.*

I tilted my head up from a half dozed off sleep, and all I saw was legs. Beautiful legs!

My gaze turned into dazed. And while still fixated on those beautiful legs, I hear a voice say, "Sorry I woke you, are you ok?" The, *"My eyes are up here,"* in the tone of her voice, shamed me to jerk my head up to look at her face. "Hmmm," I thought, "Her face is just as pretty as her legs." With her mouth shut tight, she smiled at me with her eyes, and I think to myself, whoa, she likes me. Boy was I wrong. She took my pulse, listened to my heartbeat, turned the knob on the *"I.V."* bag, and just like that, she was gone.

Realizing it wasn't a dream, whenever she was on shift, I was on the nurse's call button like it was the joystick of a *Shoot 'Em Up* video game. I couldn't get enough *look-sees* after being hit square between the eyes with *Cupid's* arrow; something I came to find out, really pissed her off!

Her friendly, but not too interested demeanor, intrigued me. As other nurses flirted with me while listening to every diatribe I had offered, and doing their jobs with giggles and eye batting, she did her job with the discipline of a guard at the *Tomb of the Unknown Soldier.*

The more I rang, the more regimented she got in her work routine. So of course, my romantic sensibilities kicked in. I hid all her co-workers phone numbers under my pillow and concluded it was the perfect time to ask her for a date.

"Miss Nurse Paula, how about you and me go to dinner when I break out of here?"

The look on her face saying, *"What part of you rubbing me the wrong way did you miss?,"* was the perfect complement to what I was flabbergasted to hear.

In the most polite and gentle voice of an angel, she said, *"Besides you adding 10,000 steps to the walk count on each and every one of my shifts - you're a baseball player, Italian, and you have a little "Black Book" that I could use as a step stool. NO! THANK! YOU!"* she said. *"Date one of those girls that put their makeup on with boxing gloves that have been lining up outside your door. I ain't ever asking you for your autograph!"*

OMG! How can she do that with that damn, cute, fall in love with her, smile in her eyes? I liked her even more!

Then, as she strapped the blood pressure cuff on to my bicep, I could barely hear her murmur to herself, *"Good Hell, I'm not out in Left Field."*

"Wonderful!" I thought; she knows something about baseball.

Right when it looked like *Cupid's* arrows had no aim, this happened. Without notice or heads up, on the day I was to be discharged, Miss Nurse Paula shows up unprompted by the call button. "Alright!", I thought. I finally won her over.

"The doctors ordered an enema, bend over," she said. "WTF?" I almost shouted. *"An enema! You got to be kidding me! It's an elbow injury for God's sake. Why?"* I demanded.

You know how a horse does that outboard motor noise thing by flapping their lips while blowing spit out their mouths? I call it the *Mr. Ed's.* (Google it) Picture Miss Nurse Paula doing that to perfection, followed by her saying, *"Because . . . You're Full of Shit!"*

Oh, the shame!

The guilt of my bashfulness and the unease of being forced to *moon* the girl I had been courting for the last week was just what the matchmaking gods needed.

She removed her *Playtex Gloves*, pulled her pen from behind her ear, then to my delight, grabbed my hand instead of the clipboard chart, and wrote her phone number on the palm of my hand. *"If that ends up in your Black Book,"* she said, *"The answer is NO!"* And off she went.

It was obvious to me. Anybody that could take that much shit from me, I ought to marry.

So, I did.

MAMMA MIA

(BABY JESSICA'S FIRST WORDS)

I don't know the first words I spoke trying to leave my goo and gaa sounds of babydum behind. Surely it must have been *ma-ma* or *da-da*. But in an Italian household, who knows? We Italians talk with our hands as much as we do with our mouths. Even when our hands are full.

My mom, in her favorite house dress and apron, with a wooden spoon in one hand, and a glass of wine in the other, could gesticulate with elegant coordination, as if she was the maestro conductor of a philharmonic orchestra, complimenting every word she said with her arms, hands, and fingers waiving away, never spilling a drop of wine.

There is an eloquence to the Italian hand gestures, and in a culture that prizes oratory, nothing elevates boring rhetoric more swiftly than playing charades while talking out loud. To Italians, gesturing comes naturally.

Some gestures are simple.
- The side of the hand against the belly means hungry.
- The index finger twisted into the cheeks means something tastes good.
- And tapping one's wrist is the universal sign for *hurry up.*

And the classic: your 4 fingers pinched against the thumb forming a pinecone shape, pointing straight up, while shaking your wrist in a stair step motion, demanding to whoever is watching, "*GET A CLUE!*

My favorite? The flipping of the back side of your fingertips up along your neckline, then flinging your hand, open palmed, off the base of your chin, with a smirk on your face.

It's a gesture which has many meanings. But let's face it, the truth be known, it is the Italian's polite way of flipping you *the bird*. It's the perfect response to that irritating combination of an eye roll and verbal "*WHATEVER*" we all get from those snaughty nose, pant wearing below the crotch, never speak in a full sentence, teenagers.

Babies always start to communicate with hand gestures long before they start speaking, giving creditability to my Uncle Geno's hypothesis, everyone is born Italian. Whether it be arms stretched out to be hugged, clinched face and fists for a poo, or the kicking of their legs to say, "Move me somewhere else;" all us parents get the message being communicated by our little angels.

But it was our little baby girl, Jessica's first words, that I remember most. And when you hear the story, you will too!

Living 300 miles away, my Mom and Dad finally scheduled their first trip to see their new granddaughter. A happy little baby who was fresh off of winning,

"*Prettiest Eyes,*" "*Prettiest Hair,*" and overall "*CUTEST BABY*" at the *Washington County Fair.*

To prepare properly, my wife decided the guest bedroom and bathroom needed a do-over. The question at hand? Wallpaper or paint?

My wife wanted wallpaper, but since I was designated to be the cheap labor, I wanted to make the project much easier and quicker by simply slapping on a coat of paint. Lucky me, we decided paint it is! A light peach color to be specific.

You know, I truly hate shopping. Especially when the decision of what we are buying has already been made. But let me confess, I found it to be quite enjoyable, and dare I say exhilarating, to be an accomplice to picking out the accessories, and watching Paula coordinate the look. So much so, I remember having the thought on the way home; "Oh my! Except for the sex, I might be gay."

Getting a baby, a 5-year-old, plus 6 bags of decorating accessories, with a gallon of peach paint from the driveway into the house in one trip, was just the challenge a *macho man* type guy like me was looking for.

Paula tended to our son and 4 of the larger bags of the *Bed, Bath, and Beyond* trimmings. With three of the fingers on my left hand, I grabbed the paint by that flimsy wire handle on the can, used my other two fingers to hoist the remaining two shopping bags, then boosted little baby Jessica up into my arms with my right hand and arm.

"Alright, I've got this," I murmured under my breath.

Turning the key, then pushing the front door open with my foot, I squatted with a deep knee bend and simultaneously tried to put down Jessica with a soft landing, feet flat on the floor, while setting the bags and the can of peach paint down too. Just as I started to elevate my posture into an upright position, damn if I didn't start prematurely waving my arms and talking with my hands, tipping the paint can over, springing the lid, and spilling the peach paint onto our brand new, chocolate colored shag carpeting. (*Yeah, I know. . . brown shag carpeting, how ugly!*) But it was a thing back in 1982.

With a tirade of "*F*" bomb phrases, and the hand movements of an outraged mime, I started the cleanup. It was a 4-hour job, but I got it done!

What once looked like chocolate pie alamode with peach ice cream melting on top, now was back to the original, brownie brown color, and soft to the touch of your toes. The carpet looked like new.

That weekend the bed and bath areas got painted and were ready for Grandma and Grandpa's visit.

My parent's arrival was festive. As soon as the front door opened, everyone's arms and hands were flailing away, and our motor mouths shifted into high gear. We gathered like a gaggle of *Chatty Cathy's* and moved around like a five-year old's tap dance recital where no one knew their marks.

As my Mom sat on the couch and held her precious grandbaby by her hands, jiggling her arms, and bouncing her up and down with her knee, it wasn't more than a couple of *coochy - koos* in, when by the prompting of my Mom to get Jessica to say the least little resemblance to *ma-ma* or *pa-pa*, Jessica stops her giggling sounds, and with the clarity of *Professor Henry Higgins* in *'My Fair Lady,'* pronounces out - - *"FUCKING PAINT!"*

All heads turned towards me. All sounds went silent. All movement stopped. Except for Jessica! She just kept going on and on. Not once, not twice, but like an old-time record player when the needle hits a scratch, she just kept repeating it. *"F -- ing paint. F — ing paint! F — ing paint!"* Over and over and over again.

"Good God! Please make her STOP!" I silently prayed.

We had been trying for months to get our little doll face, with the most delightful disposition, to say something cute. Instead, I turned her into a female *Richard Pryor.*

Out of the mouth of babes!

Ever since that day, even the garage gets wallpapered.

A CHARLIE BROWN THANKSGIVING

It makes me sad when I find out the world doesn't think like me. And it happens so often, you would think I would grow accustom to disappointment's face. It's not the, "*I want to cry,*" kind of disappointment. Rather, it's more like when I was a kid, finding out under the tutoring of my best friend, how babies are made, and I, perplexed by the discovery, would think in my high-pitched voice out loud . . . "It's not a stork? NO! Not my parents! They wouldn't do THAT!" - kind of sad.

When that kind of gloom happens, there I will stand, mentally flat on my back, washed in confusion, like *Charlie Brown* after *Lucy* moved the football.

Imagine how I felt when I learned Italian Thanksgivings are different from yours. I never thought they were when I was growing up. I thought everybody celebrated that good old late November day of thanks like we did. In fact, I thought everybody did everything like we did. Which by design, is one of the many built in detriments of being raised by parents who worked hard daily to make us think the bubble we were raised in was the norm.

Now that I know better, and believe me, this is a hard pill to swallow, it makes me "*Charlie Brown Sad*" to know Uncle Geno was telling a fib when he would say in his old, cigar marinated, raspy broken English, "*You-a- know -a- Marko,* there are two type of people in the world - - - Italians, and those that want to be Italian!" I always believed that to be true. Little did I know.

And of all people, it's my wife, who through 43 years of marriage, gladly thanks God at night in her bedtime prayers, albeit she married one, she is all too happy not to be one.

My wife is a born and raised *Clearfield-ite,* a small bedroom community North of Salt Lake City. She is a pioneering Utah woman. Raised to enjoy the Utah staples of *Green Jell-O,* and *Funeral Potatoes.* A gal who is humble, modest, unassuming, and reserved, who rings true to the first amendment of her personal constitution, *"Always keep your words soft and sweet, just in case you have to eat them."* Isn't it obvious we were made for each other? We are so much alike!

So, I thought after 4 years into our marriage, Paula would be the perfect candidate to tell me if there is a difference between the traditional Italian Thanksgiving Day family dinner at my parent's house, and what was going to be our first Thanksgiving Day meal together at our newlywed home.

"Honey," I said. "We'll be here this year instead of there. What do you remember about Thanksgiving at my house that might be different from the Thanksgiving Dinner we are going to celebrate this year?"

My wife, a.k.a., *"Miss Mild Mannered Molly,"* morphs herself into a female version of *Colonel Jessop* in the court room of *'A Few Good Men'*, demanding I handle the truth.

"Number one," she said. "We had to eat at your house or be excommunicated. Number two! We ate on a pool table and ping pong table that was pushed together, and out of 53 people, me and your son were the only one's not trying to talk at the same time. And three! The only time in 12 hours all 53 people stopped arguing was during the 30 seconds when grace was being said. Next time I'll say a Rosary. Twenty minutes of silence in your house could win me a lot of money with your neighbors!"

"And who the Hell eats for 12 hours anyway?"

"Anything else?" I asked in an apologizing tone.

"Oh yeah, I almost forgot," was the reply. "I liked the *Lasagna, Florentina Steak, Stuffed Peppers, Ribollita, Antipasto, Veal Parmesan, Meatballs, Tiramisu, and Cannoli.*"

"Lasagna? What about the Turkey?" I asked. "Everybody thinks of Turkey on Thanksgiving. If Thanksgiving was a country, a turkey would be on the national flag."

"Look," she said, "Out of 15 feet by 6 feet of food, there is only one thing, once a year, during one meal, that doesn't have sauce, cheese, and garlic on it at your Mother's house. That's the Thanksgiving Day Turkey! It's easy to forget. I will admit though," she went on, "It's the only wine-soaked turkey I've ever tasted."

"I'm glad you can still laugh about it," I said with relief. "I thought you were mad."

Pronouncing each word slowly and distinctly like she was talking to a person who was hard of hearing, Paula said, "I'M. NOT. MAD!" She went back to her normal sweet-sounding voice and continued on. "It's just that you and your family can't believe there are people on this planet that have a Thanksgiving Dinner with dressing, gravy, yams, and pumpkin pie, all while sitting still in their chairs, and speaking five out of five sentences in English."

"YAMS???" I groaned. "Nobody eats yams!"

"You asked," she said. "It's my chance to pipe up and chime in. See, your family is rubbing off on me."

My face formed itself into a perfect oval, like a circle that had its two sides tightly compressed by a *Thigh Master.* And with my eyes silently screaming the word *"WHOA!",* I asked, "What will we do this year? Can you at least make a few stuffed peppers with marinara sauce?"

"NO!", she hollered. "I want the kids to see the normal way to eat Thanksgiving Dinner. There will be no *"Hoo-Ha"* or *"Hullabaloo"* just to find the cranberries. I want to go to the bathroom without being afraid of being hit by swinging arms and waving hands in every direction. "Let's try it my way this year," she pleaded. "Who knows? You might like it."

"No meatballs?" I asked. "NOPE!" She responded.
"No lasagna?" I tried. "NO WAY!"
"Not even the pool table?" I begged.

With her arms and hands waiving like she just became possessed by the ghost of Grandma, out comes, "NOPE! NOPE! NOPE!"

"You're not going to make Green Jell-O, are you?" I whimpered.

"*MAAAY-BEEE,*" she giggled, going back to her "*Miss Mild Mannered Molly*" voice. Then she walked over, grabbed my hand, opened it up, and placed all four of my fingers on her lips.

GREAT! I thought. Pre-Thanksgiving dinner sex. I like this custom!

As if I could no longer hear the words coming out of her mouth, she presses my fingers up against her mouth, and enunciates with over exaggerated lip movement the words; "PLEASE PASS THE YAMS," then drops my hand, and says, "Now you try it."

Good grief! I hate being a Charlie Brown.

AMORE MIO

My favorite place I have never been is *"The Copacabana."*

Here's why.

In 1940 the *Copacabana* was the "*it*" place where New York City's finest came for an unforgettable night out in the city. All the big celebrities of the time made their debuts at the *Copacabana*, everyone wanted to be a part of "*it*."

Along with the headliner talent of *Frank Sinatra, Dean Martin,* and *Sammy Davis Jr.,* the club was also known for its chorus line, *"The Copacabana Girls,"* who had pink hair and elaborate sequenced costumes, mink panties, and fruited turbans. *Barry Manilow* got it right. "Who could ask for more?"

On a non-descript Tuesday night, in walks my future Dad, who was, as the story has been told, a regular patron and known to all to be quite the dancer. In his three-piece, pin stripe, Italian tailored suit, and flashy *'SPATS'* covering his shoes, the most beautiful girl in the club, caught his eye from the horseshoe booth across the room.

A lady so stunning, she even held the envy of the *"Show Girls."*

But it wasn't my Mom. My future Mom was in the same horseshoe booth with that knock down gorgeous, eye catching gal, but sitting in the part of the booth that had her back face the entrance of the club. My Mom, along with her three best friends, and dressed to the nines, had just been seated by the *Maître' d* and ordered their first round of high balls.

Their weekly custom of girl's night out partying was just getting ready to shift a gear. It was the spitting image 1940's version of the television show *'Sex and the City'*, mimicking the cast of characters: *Carrie Bradshaw, Samantha, Charlotte and Miranda.*

I always pictured my Mom to be a *Carrie* type. Too smart, too pretty, too much attitude, all while being too much Italian. As all who knew her, then and now, my Mom was a one woman focus group. Yet, all agreed, it was my Mom's best friend, the blond bombshell of the group, the Miss, "*I'm too sexy for my skirt,*" the one that caught my Dad's eye, that was the "*man magnet*" for the table; thus, she was handpicked to always be front and center, facing the entrance door.

My Dad, whose stride was a dance move in and of itself, made his move.

According to my Dad's calculations, his style, grace, and charm would insure the next dance song, to be sung by Dean Martin, would be the beginning of his and the pin up girl's, (who my Mom later identified as a "*floozy,*" but today, would be known as the "*girl next door*"), long night of romance.

Because my Mom's back side was facing my Dad's approach, she had no idea her life was about to change forever.

Just as my Dad arrived and started to form, "May I have this dance," on his lips, to be directed to the newest girl of his dreams, my Mom turned her head over her left shoulder, looked up, and gazed straight into the eyes of my Dad.

Without pause or hesitation, my Dad, as if planned by *Cupid* himself, extended his hand, didn't even ask, and whisked my Mom off to the dance floor, or so he says.

My Mom told it differently.

She said, being the quick study that she was, "She wasn't interested in dancing with a want-to-be "*Don Juan,*" who had just stumbled into making eye contact by mistake. And with an Italian woman / New York state of mind, mumbled loud enough to hear, "*Non mi freghi!*" (you can't fool me)

Only from the kicks under the table from her friends, combined with the half rolling of their eyes saying, "Are you nuts? Dance with him," did she finally give in to his Hollywood smile and puppy dog eyes, begging for this treat.

As good as dancer as my Dad was, my Mom's recollection states, she was better. And every time the story was told, she made it clear she thanked God it wasn't a "*slow dance.*"

Once the music stopped, with a polite smile and thank you, my Mom's goal was to shake loose before the spell of the *Copa's* renowned sweet talker could take hold; so, of course, she headed for the *Powder Room*. Not to be denied, my Dad followed her in, waited outside the stall, and made his argument for all to hear as to why he needed more face time.

Because no one has ever witnessed it since, legend has it, that the one and only time a human being has worn my Mom down, was right there, and right then, in the *Lady's Room of the Copacabana*.

My Mom gave in to my Dad's plea and joined my Dad at his reserved table.

Part of the charm of the Copacabana was the nightly routine of celebrating a birthday, an engagement, or retirement of someone in the audience by incorporating their celebration into the headliner's act. But on this particular night, not one couple in the place had anything to celebrate.

The *Maître d*, in a panic of not having a celebrant couple to fulfill the *Copa's* custom, and with Dean *Martin* looking on confused as to why the delay, he approached my Mom and Dad's table with a complimentary bottle of 'Dom Perignon' with his bright idea . . . "You are the best-looking couple here tonight. Can I say it's your honeymoon and bring you up on stage with Dean?" he politely asked.

My Mom said, "HELL NO!" My Dad said, "OF COURSE!"

On stage, at the world-famous *Copacabana*, Jule and Josephina masqueraded as newlyweds, and danced their first slow dance to *"Amore Mio"* being sung by *Dean Martin*.

"Amore Mio" has been sung at every family function since, including at both my Mom's and Dad's funerals. It is our family song.

And that is how Jule and Josephina became my Mom and Dad.

Who could ask for more?

LONG LIVE MICKEY

*"If evolution really works, why does a
Mother only have two hands?"*

Milton Berle

When my son, Nathan, was around 4 years old, we
all called him *"Nate the Skate."* We called him *"Nate
the Skate"* because you couldn't blink, turn your head,
or relax for one second, without him being gone . . .
Vanished! Off to do something he figured in his mind,
couldn't possibly be the wrong thing to be doing.

Back then, we never needed gym memberships, video
work outs, or personal trainers. We just needed *"Nate the
Skate"* to be awake. If Nate was awake, we were burning
calories.

Nate would wake up each day at the first peep of
sun-up, fight tooth and nail to avoid bedtime at night, and
God forbid, if his eyes opened in the middle of that night's
sleep, the marathon of monitoring would begin at 3:00 a.m.

It was exhausting!

Trying to prove financial guru *Dave Ramsey* to be
spot on, just like many young couples at the time, my wife
and I chose to work opposite shifts in order to save a few

bucks on day care. We never did become millionaires by penny pinching as promised on the radio, and in hindsight, would have done better tuning into *"The Dr. Spock Show."*

I worked during the day, and Paula, my wife, was the head nurse of the swing shift of the intensive care unit at the hospital. And as much as I bitched and moaned about her damn, - never get off on time, - work till you drop, - make her cry, career; her crazy, long, and unpredictable swing shift hours left me and Nate home alone to hold down the fort at night.

What could possibly go wrong?

Without fail, one of us, or both of us, would always come up with a bright idea to stymie the boredom. After an hour-long meandering game of *"Hide and Seek,"* *"Nate the Skate,"* without halt or hiatus, thought it would be fun to watch popcorn pop without the lid on.

So, we got our old-fashioned popcorn popper, you know the kind; it had a plug in, bowl shaped, hot plate on the bottom where you put the oil and popcorn kernels in. Then you would cover it with that tall, see through, round, *Tupperware* type cover that looked like a yellow *Abraham Lincoln* top hat. And when the last kernel had popped, you simply turned it upside down, set the hot plate off to the side, and dug in for the good eating.

Nate was really excited to see popcorn pop with no boundaries. And it sounded fun to me too. It was unanimous. The *"Ayes"* won the vote!

But what started off with us standing back and laughing out loud while watching a volcano of popcorn explode one pop at a time, soon would morph into a game where I would pay "*Nate the Skate*" a nickel for every piece of popcorn he caught in his mouth while he rode his tricycle in a circle around the dangerous, uncovered, scalding oil holding hot plate.

We had a lot of fun! Nate filled his *Piggy Bank,* and most important, we never got caught. And the reason why we never got caught is because the last thing I said to Nate every night before I tucked him in and kissed him good night, no matter the escapades, was, "DON'T TELL MOM!" And "OK Dad!" Was always his final answer.

Until this happened . . .

After playing indoor baseball with a broom handle and a ball made out of socks, it was time for bed. It was a great game. Nate won 6 to 3, and on that particular night, we hadn't broken anything, so we both considered it a win for the home team.

But the fun times turned foul.

We had this rule in our house that you had to "*straighten up*" your bedroom before you went to sleep. And just like every other kid on the planet, Nate refused to buy into the "*Cleanliness is next to Godliness*" credo of my generation.

Every time it was time for Nate to clean his room, he would start lollygagging around with one of those stupid,

"*WHATEVER*" looks on his face, swaying back and forth, dragging his leg, trying to prolong the inevitable.

But not that night! That night was worse.

"*Nate the Skate*" turned into "*Nate the Sloth,*" performing his "*ball and chain*" pulling parade, with an exaggerated heavy dose of drama in his attitude.

Nate starts whining, making faces, and moping around, acting like a cast member in an episode of '*Drunk History*' on the *History Channel*, and then, just to really piss me off, pulls out his first, Marine family forbidden, "*Eye Roll.*"

By-the-way; that was "*Nate the Skate's*" first, and last, "*Eye Roll.*"

ENOUGH WAS ENOUGH! I hate eye rolls!

(Now let me stop the story here to say, we Italians believe, even though there is ample evidence to the contrary, that overreacting is the proper way to make a point. And according to Doctor Luigi, very therapeutic.)

Back to the story.

So, I storm into Nate's room and started throwing his toys back on to the shelf where they belong. I stepped on, and picked up, a couple of hundred '*Tinker Toys*' and '*Lincoln Logs*', shoved them back into that cheap ass cardboard tube they come in, and in one last overreacting effort to bring home my point, I grab his little *Mickey Mouse Bookshelf* with *Mickey Mouse's* head bolted into the top, and with all my might, throw it straight up into the air.

It was one of my best fastballs.

The damn thing hit the ceiling right square between the 2x4 beams, pierced the sheet rock, magically turned to just the right angle, and stuck in the ceiling because *Mickey's* ears were now holding on for dear life. A half inch either way, and it would have hit one of the wood beams and ricocheted back to the floor. But NO! This thing gets stuck in the ceiling with *Mickey's* feet, that were screwed into the bottom of the bookcase, dangling away in mid-air as if *Mickey* was still alive.

I thought, "Good job Mark!" I was sure I made my point. This *"Dad Tantrum"* would finally allow me to scratch the, *"Keep your room clean"* lectures, off my parenting bucket list.

I remember having pause right then and there, worried that I might have overdone it a bit, thinking I probably scared little *"Nate the Skate"* to death.

NOPE!

When I turned around, expecting to see Nate moments away from a full-fledged cry and the fear of God on his face; I instead see him standing there, strategically stationed in the doorway for a quick getaway, looking at me with his cute, genuine, happy smile, and a little halo over his head as if he was just touched by an angel.

I think, "What the HELL?!"

And in my sternest, *"I'm The Dad, You're Not"* voice, I look Nate straight in the eye and say . . . WELL?

In Nate's cutest, innocent, and most pure joy tone, he says, "Boy, mom's going to be mad at you when she gets home!" And off he skipped, singing *"It's a Small World After All."*

When Paula got home, all I got was another eye roll.

Unlike Nate, it wouldn't be her last.

RUDOLPH'S RED NOSE

With only days left till Christmas, I must tell you this. There is a communist plot developing. No American is immune. It is designed to hit us all. You're probably next!

I tried to put my grandchildren's Christmas toys together last night. This is when it became clear to me. Those lousy flag-burning, *John Wayne* hating, never eat apple pie, hate baseball, pinko commies have linked into the American toy market.

I'm sure of it!

It's not their *KGB*, it's not that pain in the ass *Vladimir Putin's* election tampering, nor is it their nuclear arsenal. No folks, instead, it is tens of thousands of secretly trained Russians who have masterminded their way into the instruction sheet department of all the major toy companies. Their goals qualify for a special page in the famed "*Russian Manifesto.*" The plan will set us up for an easy take over!

This is how I figure, they figure, it should work.

Each special agent is instructed to, at all costs, – remove the most important screw for assembly out of every instruction packet, – leave #5 too light to read on the necessary direction sheets, and without fail, – make sure the customer will need the equivalency of a *John*

Deere assembly line for tools. Then, to ice the conspiracy theory cake, use only lawyer's English so that unless you are capable of landing the *Space Shuttle* on the *Heli-Pad* at the *University Medical Center*, you are forced to guess at what you are doing.

Oh yeah, I almost forgot. Never! Never ever! Give the customer batteries!

Those un–American, no hot-dogs, quiche eating, steroid using, can't beat '*Rocky*' in a fight, Russians have studied our holiday habits closely. Their special reports show that 98 percent of all parents in America wait until Christmas Eve between 10 p.m. and 2 a.m. to assemble the next morning's goodies of joy. And of course, there is no store or *Ace Hardware* open within 100 miles for quick relief. Not a nut, not a matching screw. Even *7-11* is out of *Triple A batteries*.

Now I've got a rocking horse that won't rock, an air hockey game with no air, a soccer set *Pele'* himself couldn't put together, and a wife who has carried on a 40-minute conversation with the *"Elf on the Shelf."*

After 4 hours I looked like *Bruce Willis* in the heating vent of the movie '*Die Hard'*. With bloody hands and feet, sweating like a constipated elephant, I started murmuring; "It will be fun". . . "Some assembly needed". . . "Yippie Ki Yay M#%@&*fer!"

I was wiping my nose on my sleeve, my eyes looked like they were propped open with toothpicks, and I was speaking through gritted teeth. Five more minutes and I would have started foaming at the mouth! It was terrible!

You see, it is part of their plan. That's when they'll hit. Late Christmas Eve, 400,000 Russian agents will waltz in with straitjackets - and the sad thing is, most of us will welcome them with cookies, milk, and open arms. Because at this point, the alternative SUCKS!

Before you know it, we will all be in a *Moscow Toy Factory* making pre-assembled tanks and guns for their *May Day Parade* celebration. Pre-assembled toys would become a matter of national defense for the *Kremlin*.

So fight back America! Interrupt their diabolical scheme. Spend that extra 20 bucks for a pre-assembled bicycle. If the store clerk won't sell it to you, turn him into the *FBI*.

And be aware! That red flash in the sky on *Christmas Eve* may not be *Rudolph's* nose.

A TIP FOR TIPS

I hate being up sold. Don't you?

Upselling is a sales technique where a seller induces the customer to purchase more expensive items, upgrades, or other add-ons, in an attempt to make a more profitable sale. Everything sold today, just as the negotiation is about to end, always has one last caveat to separate you from your money.

- Fries with that Whopper?
- $400 warranty for a $600 TV?
- How about an engine rebuild while you're here for an oil change?

Or the worst; "I need to see you back in the *Doctor's Office* in 2 weeks to tell you the exact same thing I told you today because it's important for me to get another billable hour on the books.

Costco has the best upsell techniques. Free food samples! With an estimated time of arrival at around noon, it's the best variety lunch buffet in town. And for a $1.50, you get a hotdog and drink for dessert on the way out.

But albeit there is free food or drink at the end of every isle, there is an emotional price to *Costco's* upsell. Those damn purgatory length check-out lines. As I stand 14ᵗʰ in line, right next to the belly dumpster size of *Orville Redenbacher Popcorn*, I use the *Hubble Telescope* type binoculars I picked up in isle 9 to zoom in to see why the delay?

I can see the lady working at my check stand is busier than a cat trying to cover turds on a marble floor. Then I scan the landscape back and forth and notice 6 unopened lanes. And there, in the only other opened check stand, I see some guy wearing a pocket protector, ball point pens in perfect order, buying a 55 gallon drum of white out, smiling ear to ear in his *Buddy Holly* glasses, backing up overflowing shopping carts through the flowers and into the produce section.

YIKES!

Then the kicker. . . I see the assemblage of associates arguing about last night's NFL game, completely oblivious to what looks like *Moses* leading the faithful to the parting of the *Red Sea*. As children hug their mom's thighs, wailing for relief from the punishment of being stationary, I think to myself; "I can't be the only one that thinks, something isn't right here! This can't be that tough to solve!"

I've seen and heard good vibes about *Costco* being a wonderful company, how did they so terribly miss the mark on this one? Well, here's my idea. How about reducing the scheduled 214,000 pay raises by .003 cents of each employee and open another check stand? Or at the very least, move the break room to the back, out of sight, so we are fooled into thinking there isn't enough people on duty to help. Don't provide visual salt in my lack of patience wound.

My best personal upsell was for tips. My plan was so clever, so friendly, so passive; no one ever caught on. And we made a haul!

Here's how I did it.

During the off season, while living an out of money experiment, myself and my best friend landed jobs as bellman at the *Airport Holiday Inn*. Being the closest hotel to the Airport, the courtesy phone for a free ride to the hotel rang of the hook.

The job description was simple:
- Dress up in a cheap, ringmaster looking, bellman's uniform.
- Pick people and their luggage up at the airport.
- Drive them back to the hotel.
- Don't get in a wreck.

Base pay was $1.35 an hour plus tips.

So how do you upsell bellman tips? Picture this . . .

My best friend, adorned in his best 3 piece suit, sporting a business briefcase in his right hand and carrying a folded copy of *The Wall Street Journal* tucked under his left arm pit, would masquerade as a *Holiday Inn* customer waiting to be picked up as if he just came off a *Delta Airlines flight*. With one last seat available, he would be the final pick up, needing to be squeezed in for the ride. He jumps on the van and says loud enough for everyone to hear, "This is the first time I've been to Salt Lake. The mountains here are beautiful!"

Off we go!

As I steered with one hand, I clicked on the microphone of the portable *karaoke* machine I had bought earlier that morning just for the sole purpose of being heard. Then I began to bellow my scripted upsell spiel. I would tell all ears about the restaurant, the bar, *Utah's crazy liquor laws*, and a little snippet or two about *Salt Lake*.

Depending on the stop lights, it was a three to five-minute trip; so of course, I had a red-light speech and a green-light speech. Perfectly timed to finish as I pulled under the hotel canopy to the front doors of the *Holiday Inn*, I would broadcast in full volume on the microphone, "I will get your room number and drive your bags to your room!"

Jumping to his feet as if he were just *tazed,* my best friend stands up and proclaims in his loudest voice: "*YOUNG MAN, I'VE TRAVELED ALL OVER THE COUNTRY AND STAYED AT THE NICEST HOTELS. YOU'RE THE BEST DAMN BELLMAN I HAVE EVER SEEN!*" Then he pulls a *Soprano* size wad of cash out of his front pocket, rolls off about 20 one-dollar bills, and high fives me the loot as if I just hit the game winning home run!

I looked in the rear-view mirror and saw every single customer fumbling and scrambling through their pockets, purses, and wallets in search for tip money. Then it was rinse and repeat for the next courtesy bus run. Like I said, we made a haul!

Pretty good upsell, don't you think?

But if I was to do it again; free snacks in paper cup cake holders and a hot dog and a Coke for a buck and a half would be included.

ALMOST A HIT

I hate running!
Always have, always will.
But this happened...

August 1982

It's like a chain smoker trying to give up smoking - I could do it if I really wanted to - I just never wanted to run a marathon.

I always have enjoyed putting my two cents worth into a conversation and while I'm at work is just as good of time for me as any. In fact, some of my best chiming in happens when I'm getting paid. And sure enough, the "*Big Boss*" hears through the grapevine my opinion about running, (It's not so tough), and I am invited, via handwritten memo, to a meeting with only me, and a room full of the higher ups of the newspaper.

Now I know something is up because you go to a meeting --- you're not invited to them.

Most of the time, meetings are attended after receiving a non-negotiable summons. And the sole purpose of having a meeting at the newspaper was always to arm the "Big *Boss*" with ammunition to stop any argument an employee was winning by simply saying, "We talked about this in the meeting," knowing full well none of us were paying attention at the time.

I had no idea why this meeting was being called, but my mind deduced that a solo meeting with the big bosses, could very well mean, I was about to be fired.

"Hello John," I said. (General Manager John Rogers is the "*BIG Boss*")

"Hello Carrick," I said. (Managing Editor Carrick Leavitt is my boss too)

"Hello Paul," I said. (News Editor Paul Challis is another Boss)

In fact, this meeting looked like the *Spectrum's* version of *The State of the Union Address*. All the high-powered people that should be there, were there. And all the people at the newspaper that shouldn't have been there, were watching and listening through the glass sliding window in the newsroom.

"Sit down," John said.

"Thank you," I said cheerfully. Every boss likes a happy employee.

"Mark what do you think about jogging?"

"Oh, I've done it a little, usually when my girlfriend dumped me – the further I'd run, the uglier she got."

"What about a marathon?" He said.

"I was never that in love, I'd never run one of those things," I said. "Besides, I was always too busy getting ready for a tough sport, a man's sport, football, baseball, basketball. You know what I'm talking about, you went to some of the games."

"Hey now, I've been at the finish line at the last three *St. George Marathons*," John said. "People go through a lot of pain," he added, pointing out that a marathon is 26 miles, 385 yards - the distance from *Marathon, Greece to Athens* - and that the original guy who ran it, carrying the news of a war victory in 490 B.C., died of exhaustion moments after arrival.

"Well I'm not in that bad of shape!" I said. "I mow my lawn twice a week, I catch fast pitch softball, and I almost got a hit off of *Val Peterson*. That's worth a couple of miles, don't you think?"

"Besides, you ought to pitch with a sore arm and an umpire who sleeps standing up - that's pain! But with a little bit of work, I'd run a marathon, that is, if I wanted to."

"Good, good, good," John said. All heads in the room nodded in agreement.

"*The Spectrum* is one of the sponsors of the *St. George Marathon* and we feel we should have a runner represent the company. We will even buy you a cute little running outfit with 'SPECTRUM' printed on it."

In fact, added *Leavitt,* this could be an interesting story. Let people know what it's like for a novice to enter. "You can show everyone it's not that tough."

Like I said, I was sitting there within earshot of everybody. I never realized we had so many employees. This was not the time to back down.

"Sure, I'll do it," I said with a shrug. "When is this thing?"

Six weeks from now, Oct 2nd, they replied.

I wondered, when should I start training? I figured sometime in early September ought to be good enough.

As I got up to leave, I wondered to myself how come the rumor mill at the 'SPECTRUM' had never leaked back to the *"Big Boss"* anything about me deserving a raise. As usual, selective gossip bit me in the butt.

My friend Debbie is the premier female runner in southern Utah. She is also my neighbor. She has run 17 marathons, 33 half marathons, and a plethora of mini marathons. Since she started training six years ago, she has run over 3,500 miles – more miles than the length of the United States. She presently puts in more than 100 miles a week!

She tells me she considers herself an average runner.

Whoa! AVERAGE? Now I worry. The last time I heard mileage like that I was at the airport and the flight attendants were complaining about jet lag.

I explained my situation, that I have decided (was coerced) to run in the *St. George Marathon*, and I would like a few tips.

"When do we start training, September 1st? I asked.

She laughed. "The race is Oct 2nd, you should have started training a year ago."

"You've got to be kidding!", I said. "We only had two-a-day practices in football for two weeks; Ya know, we took State."

"You better start today," Debbie said.

How often do I go?

"Every day without exception." What kind of feet do you have?", she said.

"Unless they're adopted, they're *Italian,*" I said.

"No, no," she said. "You need running shoes. We've got to get you fitted. You'll hate running without the right shoes. And DON'T wear those tube socks - you're not in a basketball game."

How embarrassing! I always thought I looked *Sports Illustrated* worthy with my *Magic Johnson* sanctioned basketball tube socks.

Great, I can't wear my pretty generic no name shoes, no tube socks, and I'm late to the training table by about twelve months. I hope she doesn't notice I combed my hair.

"You need a schedule and a diet wouldn't hurt you either," she said. The more luggage in the trunk, the worse the gas mileage. Sorry Mark, your trunk is full."

This rain on my parade was turning into a flash flood. I just about said with my typical smart-ass attitude, "Hey, I gotta run," thinking that would be a cute thing to say to end a conversation about marathons. But the look on Debbie's face was a slap to my face.

This marathon thing is serious business.

"I better be going," I said. "I'm going home, turn on my music from *'Chariots of Fire'* and read the clippings in my baseball scrap book."

"Hey Debbie, do you think I can do all right in this marathon thing?"

"Sure," she said. "Don't worry about it."

She must have seen me almost get a hit off of *Val Peterson.*

Boob Job

I was half naked, sweaty clear through, and so tired I couldn't finish - couldn't keep my legs pumping - along the ribbon of asphalt snaking uphill through sun-blistered *Snow Canyon State Park*. Suddenly, running was the pits, depression's bottom line. "I can't finish! Can't Finish!" Screamed my own voice in the back of my mind.

This was a new sensation. I couldn't will myself to continue. Something I always could muster in every other difficult endeavor. Raised to gut it up, no matter what, I always thought I could force my myself to continue any task.

But this time, I hit "*The Wall*." A place I was warned about from other runners, yet arrogantly ignored, where a runner's ambition dies. (In endurance sports such as cycling and running, "*hitting the wall*" is a condition of sudden fatigue and loss of energy which is caused by the depletion of glycogen stores in the liver and muscles.) In simple words, I was DONE!

Hitting "*The Wall*" sucked all my mental motivation out of my brain, froze my physical abilities, and left me feeling like I just found out the cute girl who asked me to the *Sadie Hawkins Dance* only asked, because she had lost a bet. I stood there motionless, my mind flashed back to a collage of pictures showing my coaches, teachers, Mom & Dad, all rehearsing the cover songs of my youth.

"DON'T QUIT!"
"GUT IT UP!"
"MUSCLE THROUGH IT!"

But I couldn't do it! I didn't care! I was depleted!

I wasn't expecting this. After all, I was an athlete, who, yes, often found myself sad and disappointed because of a loss in a game or making an unforced error. But never, ever, was I depressed because I flat out quit! They all told me training for and participating in a marathon would be exhilarating. But there I stood, unable to take just one more step. Exhilarating my ass!

My mind convinced my soul, legs, and feet that I had been scammed. That this was some kind of cruel joke. A hazing initiation ritual designed specially and uniquely by the running gods to punish new members trying to join their pavement pounder club. Getting depressed about the trials and tribulations of running was not on my radar. Being soar, being achy, getting a few *"Charlie Horses;"* I was prepared for that. But depression? C'mon!

Here's how it happened to me.

Runners getting ready for a marathon have a schedule. Once a week, usually on a Saturday, the runner who is serious, goes for a *"long run."* Mine would be 20 miles – *St. George* to *Ivins*, up through *Snow Canyon*, out the top end, and back to *St. George* – running, running, and running, until reaching that 20-mile distance. Little did I know, the *'Devil of Death'* of a runner's endorphins showed up in better shape than me.

Things were great until the last 1/2 mile out of *Snow Canyon*. I got slower and slower until I hit *"The Wall"* and stopped dead in my tracks. Now I was standing on the road back to *St. George*, sweaty and half naked. I wasn't going to move another inch.

My hands were trying to negotiate a contract between my legs and brain to do something besides just stand there. I had mental yellow ribbons tied all over my body waiting for my senses to come home. I tried hitchhiking, but, would you pick up a half-naked sweat hog whose hands were talking to his feet and head? No one else would either.

I couldn't finish and there was no way to get there from here. It was depressing. And, it was depressing being so depressed. I couldn't finish, I couldn't finish, I couldn't finish! That's all I could think. It was mental gas pains and I had no *Alka-Seltzer*. Dejected and downtrodden, regret stepped up to shake my hand. I was convinced that signing up and training for the *St. George Marathon* was an embarrassing mistake.

Other runners came to my rescue. "Don't worry about it, there's still plenty of time," they said. "It was all uphill. It's your homework. You'll pass the real test! This really will prove to have done you some good," they said. They did their best to keep me positive, bless their hearts.

I did make it home much later that day via automobile after I made a search and rescue call to my wife. I lollygagged around the house, pouting around like a child who got broccoli for dessert. I was in a bad mood and blew off the efforts of my wife and kids to motivate me into happiness.

I was in a constant state of passion, thinking about my failure so often that it kept me from my food and drink. But for my wife, enough was enough!

That night, as bedtime approached, she came downstairs in what I mistakenly perceived to be her "*let's do it*" nightwear, leaned over kissed me on the cheek, pinched my butt, and said . . . "You're a BOOB! Quit being a BOOB! Your sleeping on the couch and I'm sleeping upstairs butt naked! See how not finishing that feels! SNAP OUT OF IT!"

WHOA! Who knew? I married the female version of Vince Lombardi.

Laying on the couch, after debating with myself as to whether it was good or bad, right or wrong, I fell asleep, brainwashed healthy and happy. It was as if I had decided to not enter the marathon at all.

TURN THE OTHER CHEEK

Have you ever been in a fight? I have. Once. Only one time. Here's how that happened.

ST. GEORGE DAILY SPECTRUM NEWSPAPER

Wednesday, July 6, 1983
The Making of "Wop, Wop" Marine

You know, we are a high-powered business here at the *'SPECTRUM'*. We even have two sets of bathrooms with your choice of six different ways to get to each. Yesterday, wouldn't you know it, I chose the wrong way to the wrong bathroom. I must admit, it's my favorite way - past advertising, by two secretaries, one big boss, another big boss, past accounting, through two newsrooms and you are there. It's the scenic route, worth at least ten minutes away from my desk. Needless to say, I drink a lot of water.

But yesterday, I should have been on the wagon. I was headed off at the pass; so to speak.

As I walked by the office of southern Utah's chunky version of *Perry White*, I stuck my head in to say hello and was greeted by all the big cheeses of the company.

"Hi Mark," said the Big Boss. "C'mon in and sit down, let's visit."

Well, what could I do? I went in for a chat.

"Okay, what's up here? I wondered. It's forty minutes till deadline and you guys are relaxed. Aren't we printing today?"

It looked like a party. You should have seen it. Pizza, red check tablecloth, a map with Italy circled in red, *Luciano Pavarotti* singing in the background. *The Editor* was even holding an *Italian flag.* "Something isn't right here," I said with confusion.

Forty minutes 'till deadline and this looks like a booth at the *Italian Festival*. Around here, that's like the President putting the *Red Phone* on hold. What are you guys trying to say here?

"Relax, here have a piece of pizza. What are Italians famous for?" *The Editor* asked. "What do you people do well?"

"Hey," I said snickering. "You really don't want me to say it aloud, do you?"

"No, no, no," the big boss said. "Tell me some famous Italians and what they do."

"Well boys," I said, standing with a *Fonzie* type arrogance. "We are a versatile people. We've got *Sinatra* and *Caruso* in music. *DiMaggio* in baseball, *Al Pacino* in the cinema, *Davinci* invented a whole bunch of good stuff, and my Mom's a great cook. And besides that, I think somewhere in the bible it says God is Italian. Like I said, (my arms in the air as if it were a lecture) we do it all!"

"I think of boxing," said the Big Boss. "*Marciano, Graziano, Mancini*! You guys are great boxers."

"Oh yeah, I almost forgot," said I, standing up to throw punches at the *Xerox* machine. "*Marciano* was the greatest ever. Undefeated champion you know! Even the movies knew well enough to use an Italian, there were three Rocky movies," I said braggingly.

There was excitement in the air, I was getting carried away, even started to break a sweat when they dropped the bomb: "*WE WANT YOU TO BOX AT THE WASHINGTON COUNTY FAIR AUGUST 12.*"

The music went silent, the newsroom went silent, the phones weren't even ringing. There I stood. I had taken their bait; hook, line and sinker. I'd even swallowed half their fishing pole. I looked like *Wyle E. Coyote* after the roadrunner beat him at his own game.

"What do you know about boxing," Mark?

I was still stunned. I didn't even know who asked the question. "Well, I read a *Muhammad Ali* poem once when he was still *Cassius Clay*. I know *Sugar Ray Leonard* and his kid drink *Seven Up*. And I think I can remember all the words to the *Aqua Velva* theme song. Does that count?"

"No school yard fights?" asked the Big Boss.

"Nope, private school, too many nuns," I said.

"No fights over girlfriends? asked The Editor.

"Nope, all my girlfriends wore pork chops around their neck just to get the dog to play with them. Too ugly," I said. "Look you guys, I've had a lot of things put in my face before, just none of them with some guy's fist hooked onto the other end."

"All the better," said The Editor. "Boxing is a big event at the *Washington County Fair*. Someone should let the average Joe on the street know what these people go through to put all that entertainment together on fight night. As a first timer you can really give people a taste of what it's like to train for and be a boxer."

"Let's see," I said. "Do I get a bathrobe with my name on it?"

"Yeah, sure we can do that," the *Big Boss* said.

"And do I get tassels on my shoes like on TV?" I inquired.

"Sure, sure will do it," said *The Editor*, shaking his fist in victory.

"We can even think up a catchy nickname for you."

"You can do it! You can do it!" the *Big Boss* squealed.

"You're our only Italian. It will be fun. Just think like *Muhammad Ali*," said The Editor. "Keep saying, I'm gonna whup em, I'm gonna whup em."

"Fun uh? I'll bet." I said getting up to leave.

"By the way," I said as I headed towards the door, "that ought to be, I'm gonna *"WOP"* em!"

BOX OF CHOCOLATES

I admire quick and clear thinkers. I want to be one of those! I am a *"Chute and Ladder"* thinker. When you ask me for a verbal response, strap in, you're going for a ride!

Remember the board game, *'Chutes and Ladders'?* A 3+ child's game where players try to avoid the chutes and climb the ladders to reach the final spot on the board.

You, as the character of your pawn, can see the square marked 100, but it's not so easy to get there. If you land on the right square, you can shimmy up a ladder eliminating the exercise of progressing one step at a time. But land on the wrong spot and you'll slide down a chute, having to start over to get to the finish.

Ya, well. . . That's pretty much how my brain works!

I wish I was a snappy, quick to the point thinker. I consider myself a clear thinker, but I take the scenic route of thoughts to get to the final answer. I over think EVERYTHING!

How are some people so good at quick and clear thinking? For some, every thought is quick and pinpoint perfect, always said with hardly a pause nor even a breath to collect a thought. You can tell, on their first attempt, they always say what they mean, and mean what they say.

Not me, I can change thoughts mid-sentence in order to be complicit to the reaction of the gallery. I even buy triplicate copies of the same birthday card in anticipation of my rewrites. I will rethink my thoughts ad nauseum, only to rethink them again two minutes after I have finished.

When I ask the people I later regret having asked, they tell me clear thinking is born from relaxation. Simply put, they all tell me, "I need to learn how to relax."

What is your aphrodisiac for clear thinking? How do you cleanse your thoughts to start anew? Where does your mind go to be less tense and anxious?

Some say they meditate. Others prefer the beach. Or, if you ever dated me, or happen to be the one I married, sooner or later, your clear thinking would come from infuriated and provoked, long, solo, meaningless walks. The further from me you walked, the clearer your thinking would be.

Yoga is a big deal right now. People say I should do *Yoga*. But when explained, I'm pretty sure I was raised doing *Yoga*.

It seems to me, *Yoga* is an art form exploiting the discipline of holding your body perfectly still in some odd, pretzel type contortion. Between being punished by the Nuns with an hour of kneeling in perfect praying posture on a polished wood floor, and standing in the corner, face to the wall, with the threat of, *"Don't you dare move!"* from a mother singing Italian songs, aside from the painted-on pants, *Yoga* practitioners have nothing on me.

And by-the-way, none of that was relaxing. The more the quite time, the more I needed a brain laxative. Something to clear out my clogged-up mind, cleaned and refreshed, ready to start anew.

I think clearer, crisper, and quicker, when a can of crazy has been cracked open in the midst of my calmness. Give me a fire drill, train wreck, or 60,000 chanting fans in the bottom of the 9th with the game on the line, and you will find I'm unequivocal in my thoughts. But sitting silent in an effort to relax? Not for me! Thirty seconds in and my foot would start tapping, my knee would start bouncing, and I would be like *Secretariat* waiting for the race gate bell to ring.

I blame my Mom. I never heard growing up, *"Let's chill."* My mom's version of *"chill"* was . . . "I'll give you something to cry about!" And God help me if I ever had a blank stare! You know what I'm talking about, that silent look of confusion in your eyes that happens when you have not a clue!

For my Mom, my no clue blank stares became a *Mega Hotel Vegas Casino* sign, advertising that, without immediate intervention, her son was going to *Forest Gump* his way through life, making her immediately amp up her never to be forgotten, *"Idle hands are the devil's workshop"* lecture.

How many times did you hear, *"An idle mind is the devil's playground?"*

I learned the hard way, nothing good comes from boredom. When I'm doing nothing, I think I should be doing something. When I get bored, my worst ideas get fertilized and grow into a regret. It's a Puritan ethic, or the Protestant ethic, or some such Catholic ethic, pounded into me at an early age. I was taught to feel guilty about doing nothing.

My answer? Be in a rut! Those everyday chores we all hate and are so mundane, we can do them in our sleep. Something so repetitious, it can be faked.

It must be a Dad thing. My Dad, your Dad, and their Dads, all seemed most content when being in the rhythm of a rut. I'm not sure at what age we jumped out of our personal pool of adrenaline, toweled off, and started settling for the mundane; but somewhere along the line, we found ourselves rejoicing in routine.

Now, it's the little chores in my life that clears my mind. I can combine any modest pleasure with the most mindless task and be content as can be. Dial my music list to any *Beatle CD* and I will paint the garage, re-roof the house, and cross mow the lawn just because I like the music, then, thinking quick and clear, I will come up with my best verbiage yet.

No Forest Gump stare there!

"And that's all I have to say about that."

EPILOGUE

Thank you for reading my stories. There are so many more stories for me to tell. Some are terribly tragic, and others, fantastically funny.

I encourage you to tell your stories. Share your memories.

Go ahead, take a look at the back cover . . .
Now, let me propose a toast to you . . .

- *"May you live all the days of your life."*

- *"May you have the hindsight to know where you've been, the foresight to know where you are going, and the insight to know when you have gone too far."*

- *"May we never go to Hell, but always be on our way."*

Always tell your story, don't let your ice cubes melt.

SALUTE!

Printed in the United States
By Bookmasters